POP BALLADS

CONTENTS

ISBN 0-634-03036-1

HAL•LEONARD®
CORPORATION

7777 W. BLUEMOUND RD. P.O. BOX 13819 MILWAUKEE, WI 53213

Visit Hal Leonard Online at
www.halleonard.com

PREFACE

Popular songs are everywhere. We hear them on the radio and television and in the movies. They leak from passing cars and neighbor's parties. A reflection of the times in which they were written, they become sonic time capsules that remind us of fleeting moments in our lives. This collection holds newer and older songs alike, all of them immensely popular in their time.

Playing popular songs at the piano can be a very satisfying experience. "I Write the Songs" was an important piece for me when I was a young piano student. I was really excited when I could play a song on my own piano that I heard on the radio every day. My children have that same sense of wonder about "My Heart Will Go On."

So have some fun and treat yourself to some great pop ballads at the piano!

Sincerely,
Phillip Keveren

BIOGRAPHY

Phillip Keveren, a multi-talented keyboard artist and composer, has composed original works in a variety of genres from piano solo to symphonic orchestra. Mr. Keveren gives frequent concerts and workshops for teachers and their students in the United States, Canada, Europe, and Asia. Mr. Keveren holds a B.M. in composition from California State University Northridge and a M.M. in composition from the University of Southern California.

AND SO IT GOES

Words and Music by
BILLY JOEL
Arranged by Phillip Keveren

Slowly, freely

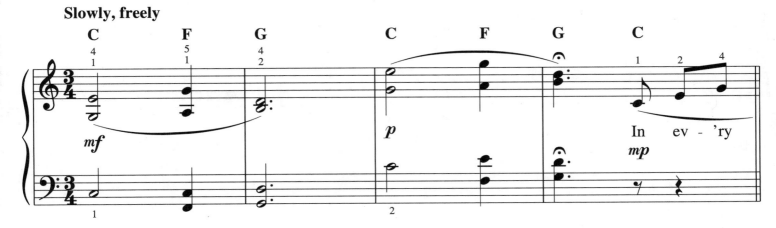

In ev - 'ry

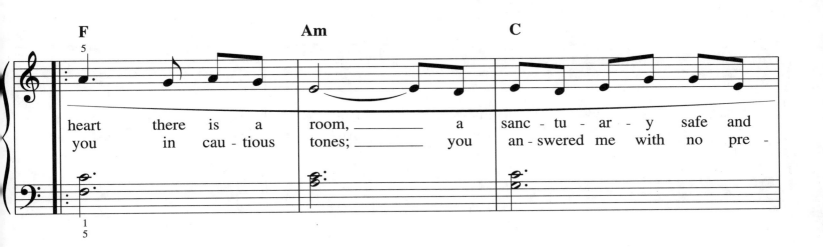

heart there is a room, _____ a sanc - tu - ar - y safe and
you in cau - tious tones; _____ you an - swered me with no pre -

strong. To heal the wounds from lov - ers past, _____ un -
tense. And still I feel I said too much. _____ My

4

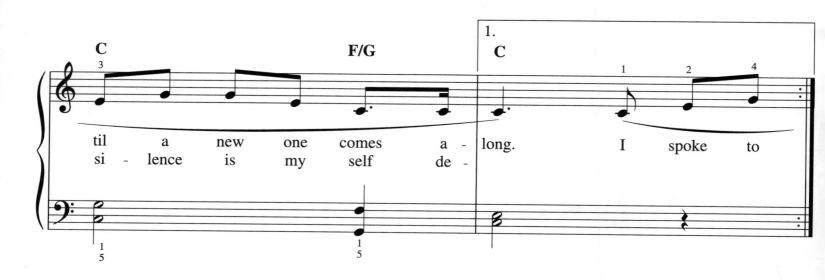

C   F/G   1. C

til   a   new   one   comes   a - long.   I   spoke   to

si - lence   is   my   self   de -

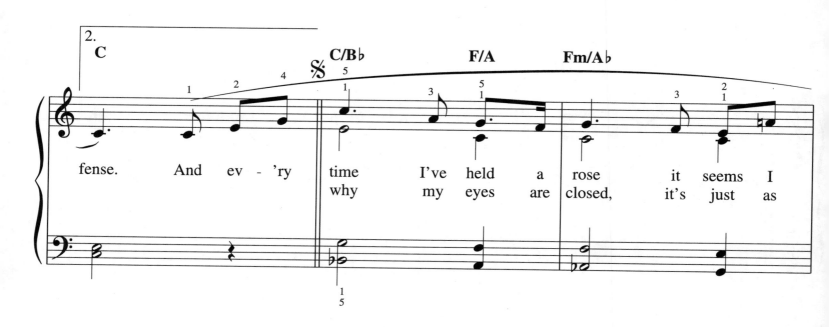

2. C   C/B♭   F/A   Fm/A♭

fense.   And   ev - 'ry   time   I've   held   a   rose   it   seems   I

why   my   eyes   are   closed,   it's   just   as

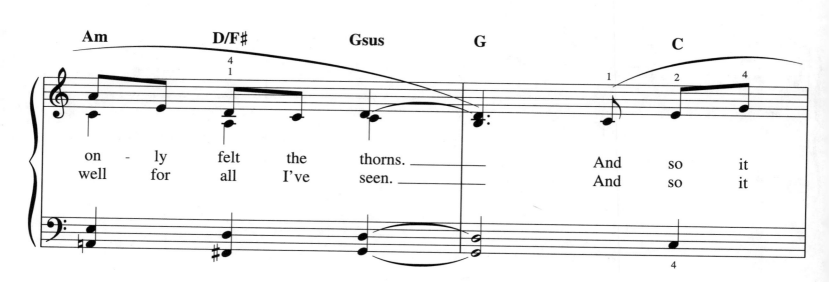

Am   D/F♯   Gsus   G   C

on - ly   felt   the   thorns. _____   And   so   it

well   for   all   I've   seen. _____   And   so   it

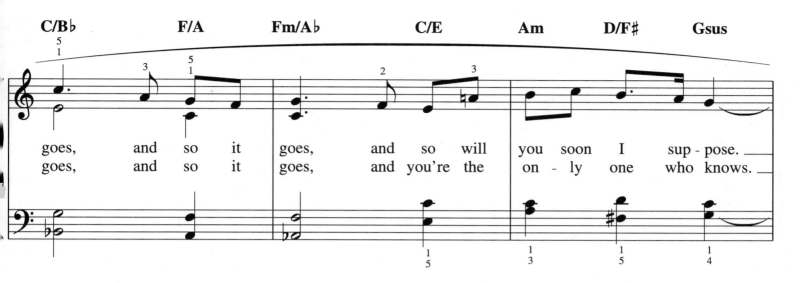

goes, and so it goes, and so will you soon I sup - pose. ___
goes, and so it goes, and you're the on - ly one who knows. ___

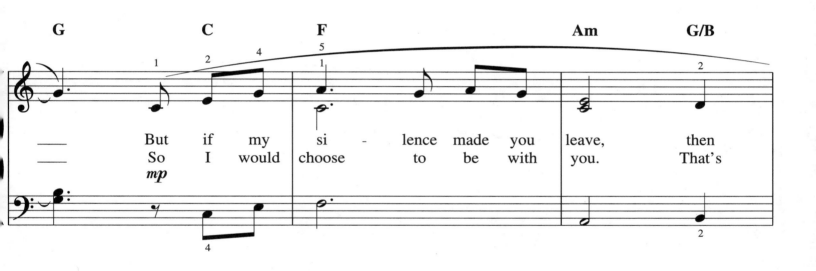

___ But if my si - lence made you leave, then
___ So I would choose to be with you. That's

mp

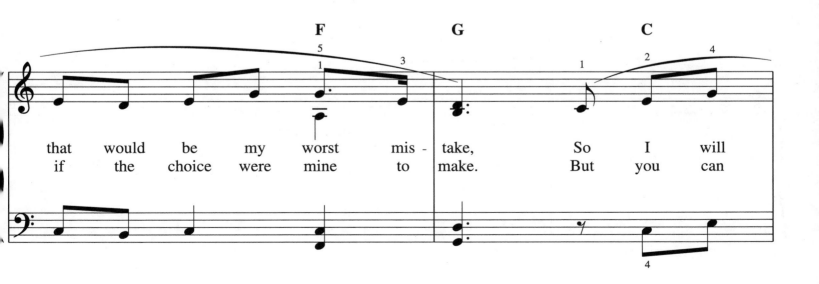

that would be my worst mis - take, So I will
if the choice were mine to make. But you can

To Coda ⊕

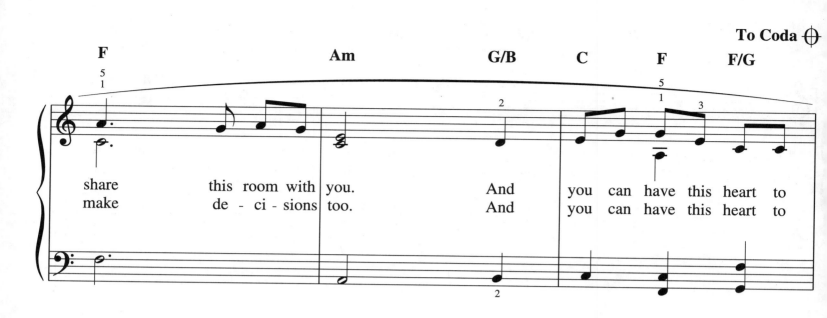

share / make this room with you. / de - ci - sions too. And / And you can have this heart to / you can have this heart to

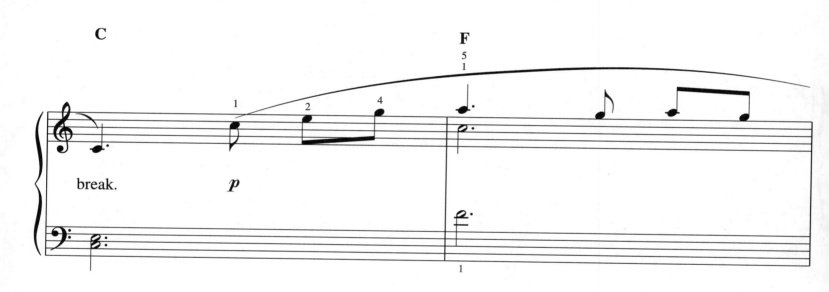

break. *p*

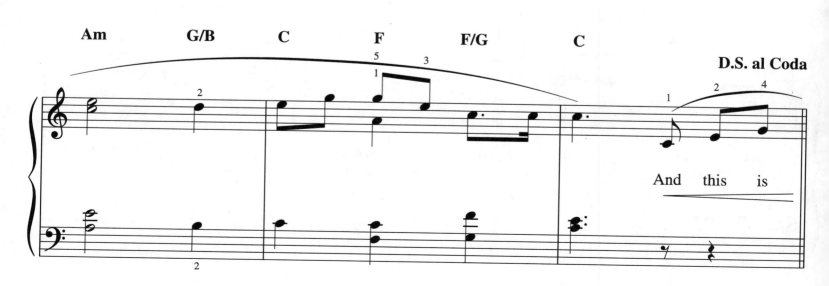

D.S. al Coda

And this is

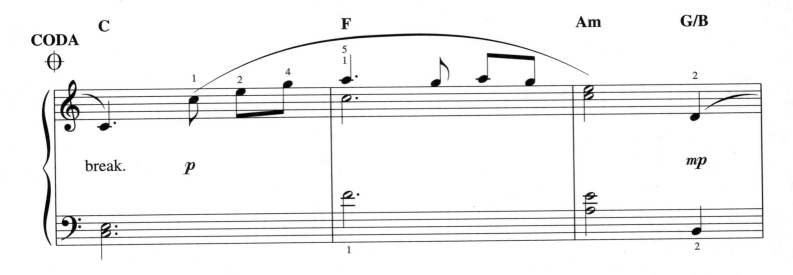

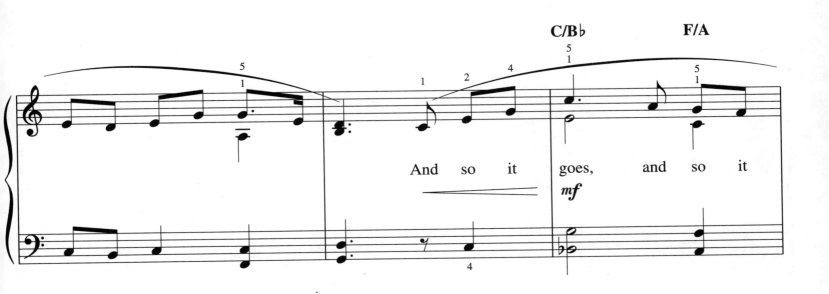

ANGEL

Words and Music by
SARAH McLACHLAN
Arranged by Phillip Keveren

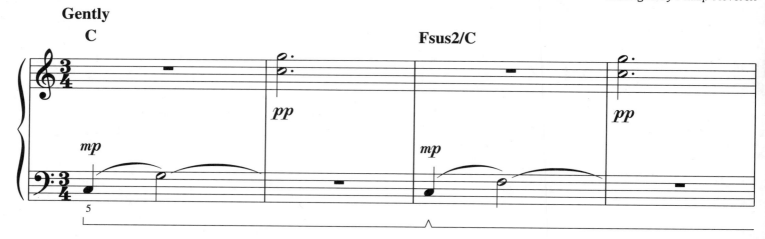

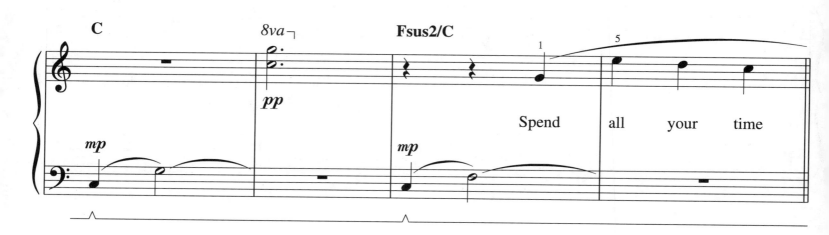

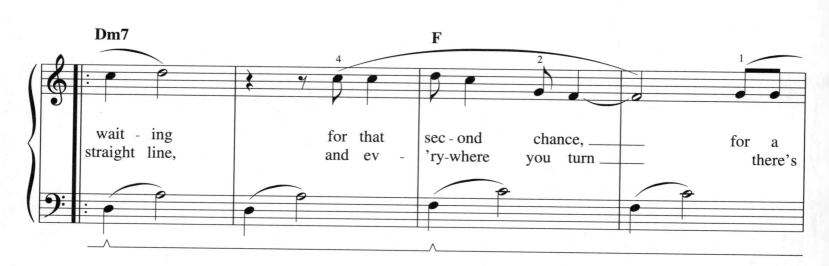

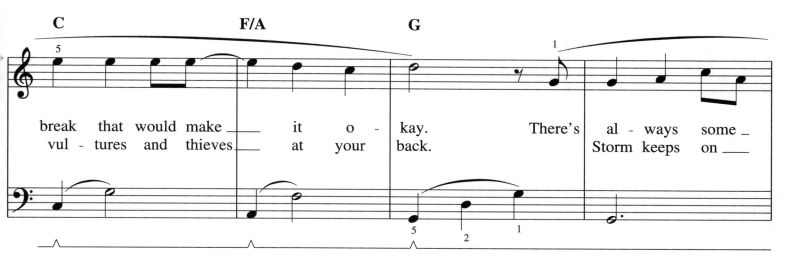

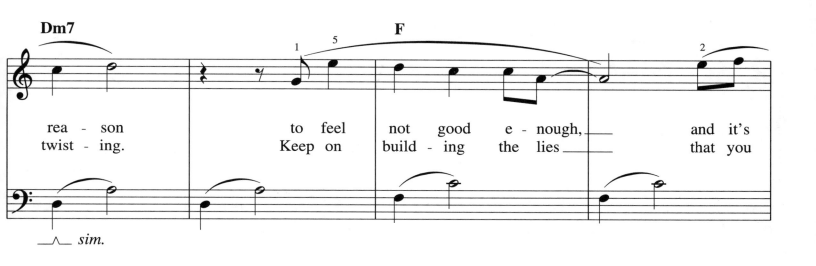

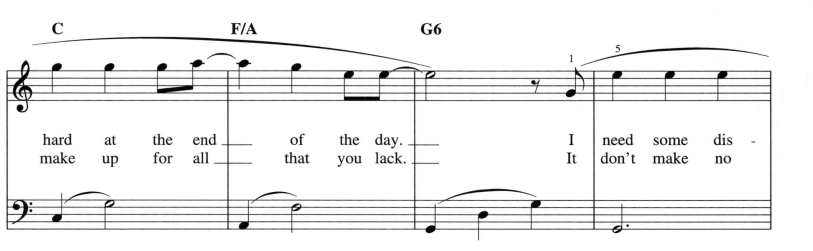

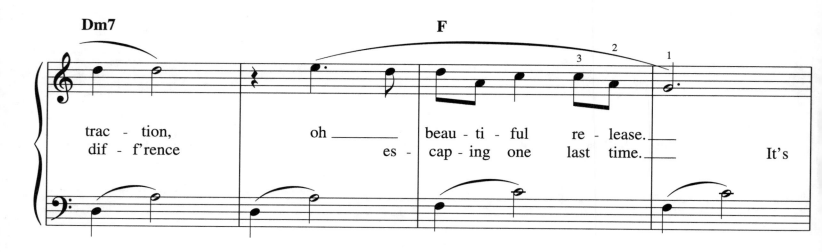

Dm7　　　　　　　　　　　　　　**F**

trac - tion,
dif - f'rence

oh _____ beau - ti - ful re - lease.___
es - cap - ing one last time.___ It's

C　　　　　　　**F/A**

Mem - o - ry seep from my veins.
eas - i - er to be - lieve

Let me be
in this sweet

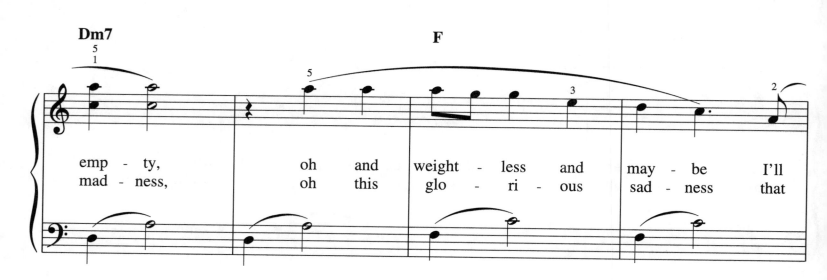

Dm7　　　　　　　　　　　　　　**F**

emp - ty,
mad - ness,

oh and weight - less and
oh this glo - ri - ous

may - be I'll
sad - ness that

DON'T CRY OUT LOUD

Words and Music by CAROLE BAYER SAGER
and PETER ALLEN
Arranged by Phillip Keveren

Slowly, in two

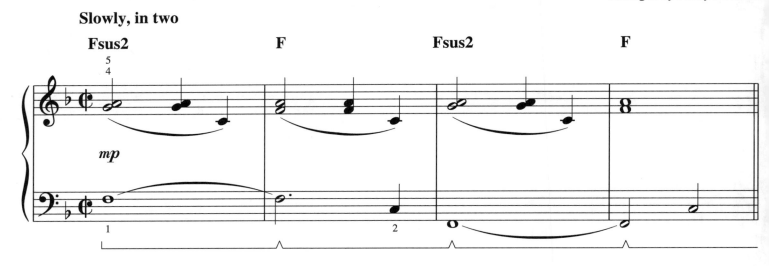

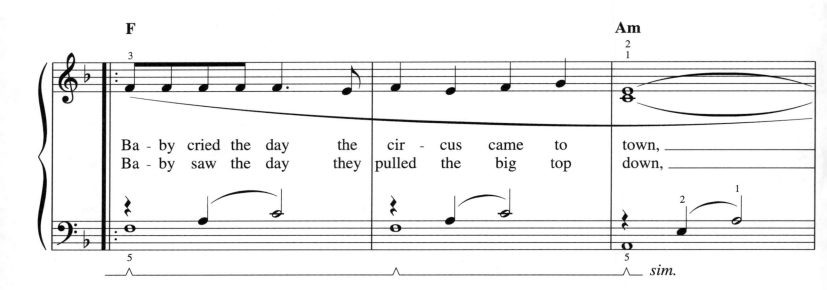

Ba - by cried the day the cir - cus came to town, ___
Ba - by saw the day they pulled the big top down, ___

'cause she did - n't like par - ades ___ just pass - ing
they left be - hind her dreams ___ a - mong the

by her. _____ So she paint-ed on a smile and
lit - ter. _____ And the dif-f'rent kind of

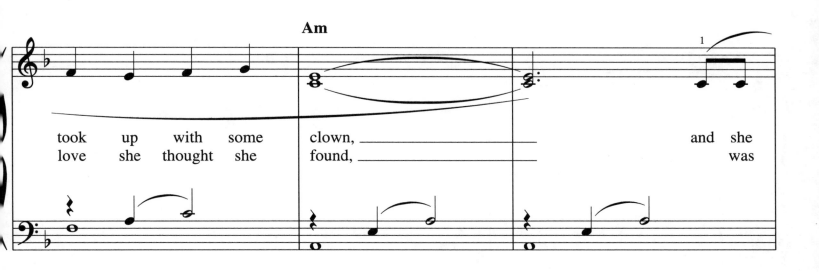

took up with some clown, _____ and she
love she thought she found, _____ was

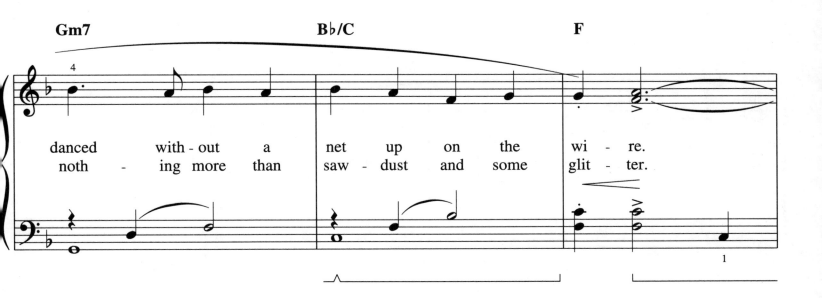

danced with - out a net up on the wi - re.
noth - ing more than saw - dust and some glit - ter.

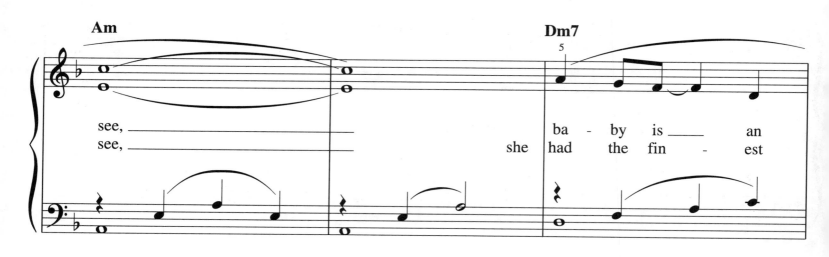

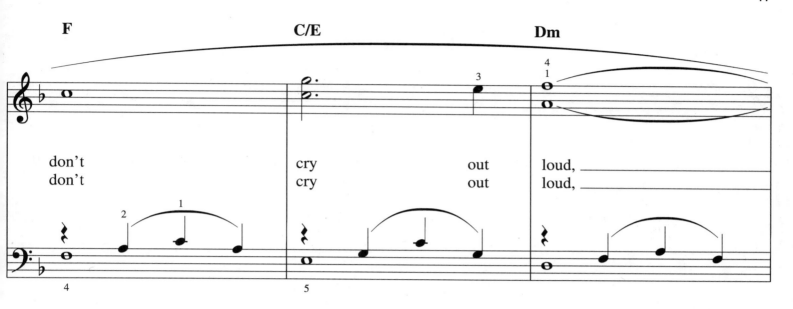

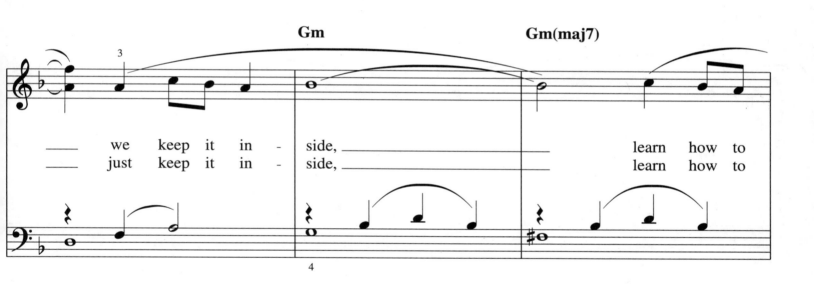

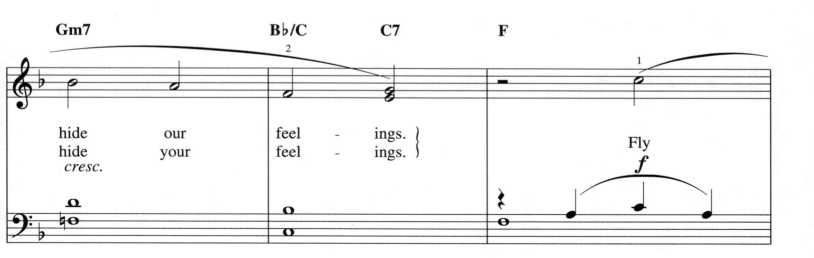

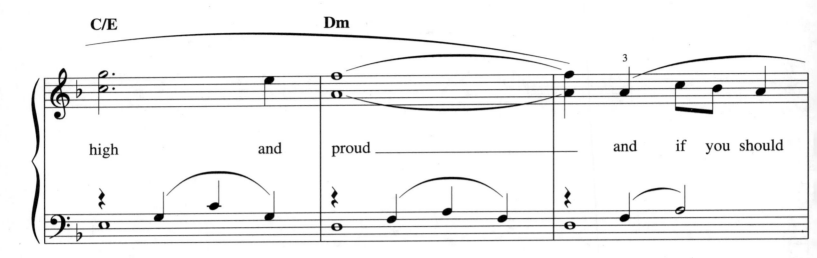

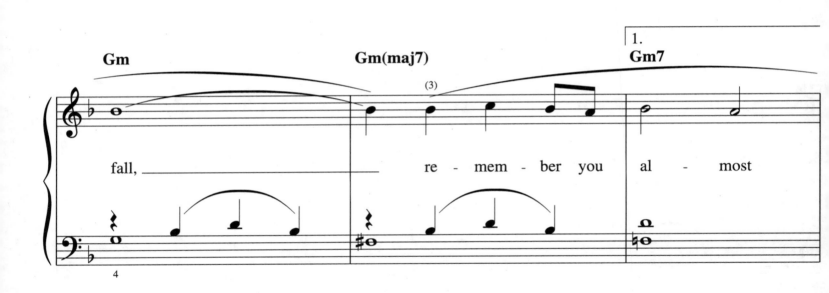

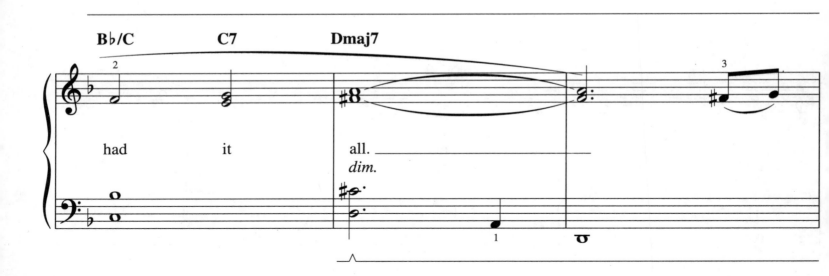

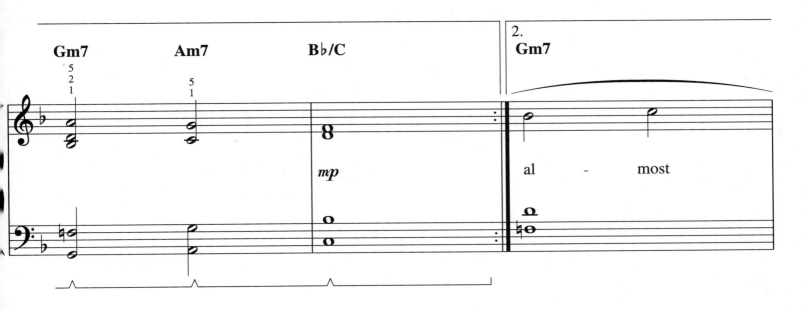

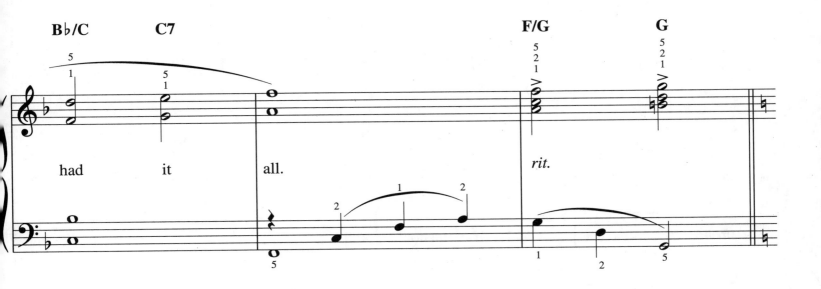

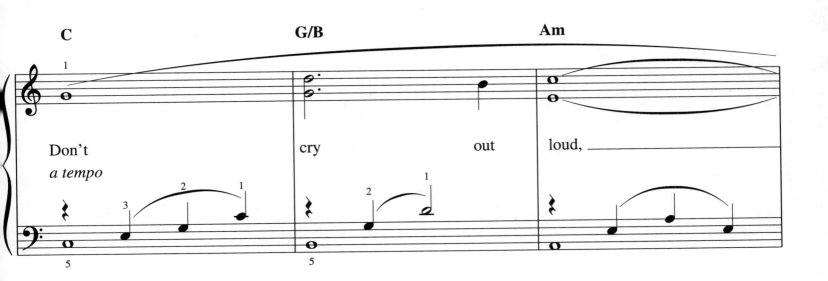

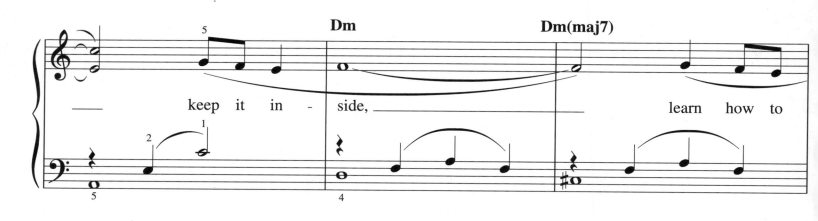

keep it in - side, _____ learn how to

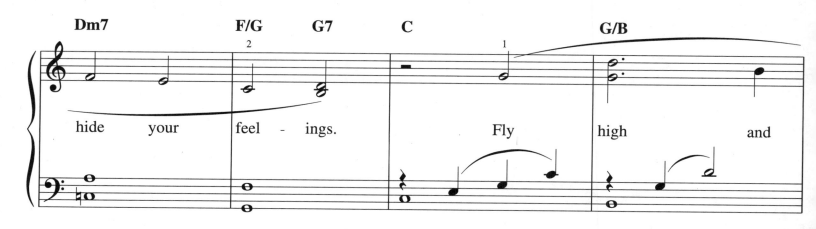

hide your feel - ings. _____ Fly high and

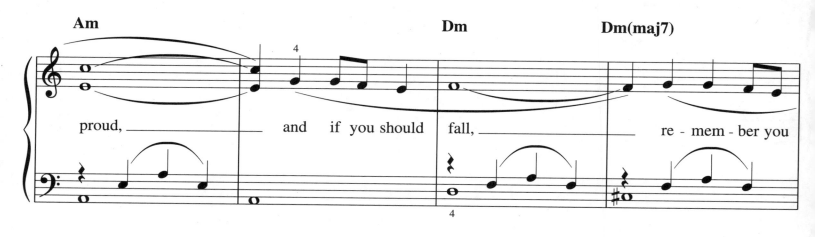

proud, _____ and if you should fall, _____ re - mem - ber you

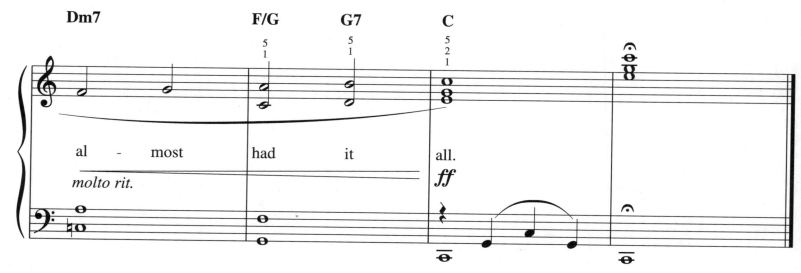

al - most had it all.

molto rit. *ff*

I HONESTLY LOVE YOU

Words and Music by PETER ALLEN
and JEFF BARRY
Arranged by Phillip Keveren

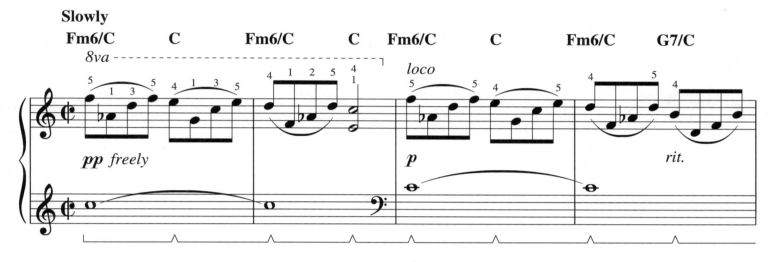

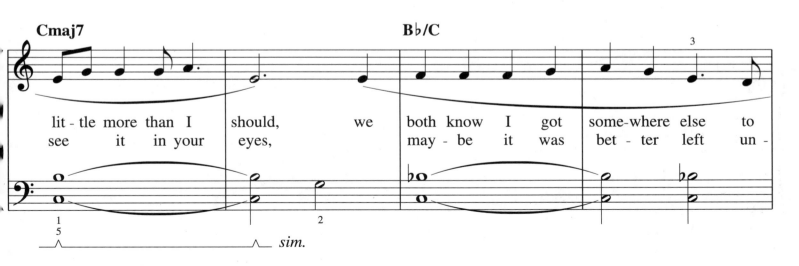

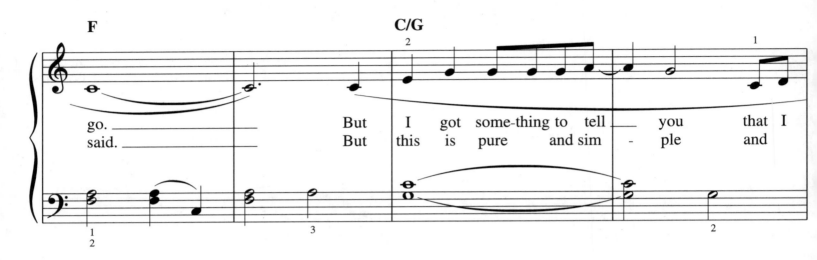

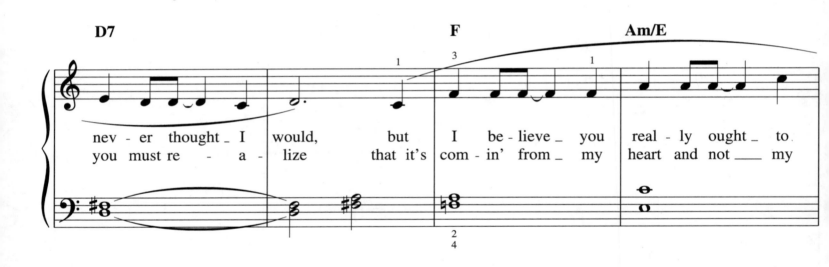

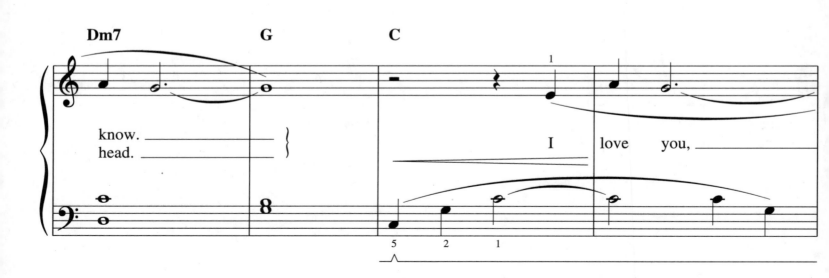

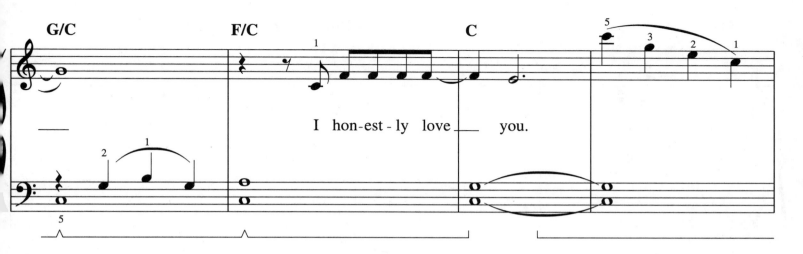

I hon-est-ly love you.

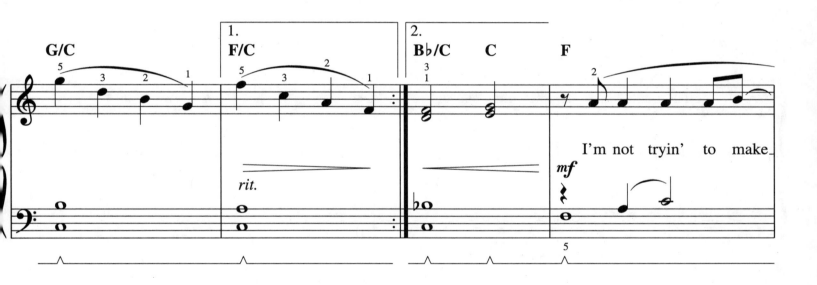

I'm not tryin' to make

you feel un-com-f'ta-ble. I'm not tryin' to make you

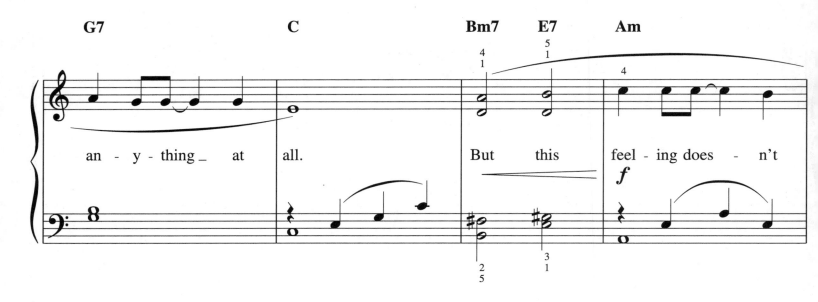

an - y - thing _ at all. But this feel - ing does - n't

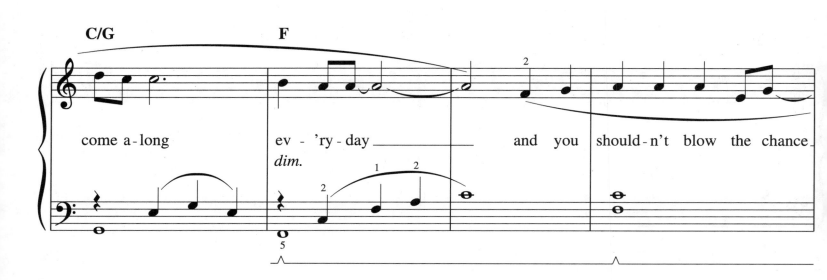

come a - long ev - 'ry - day _____ and you should - n't blow the chance _

dim.

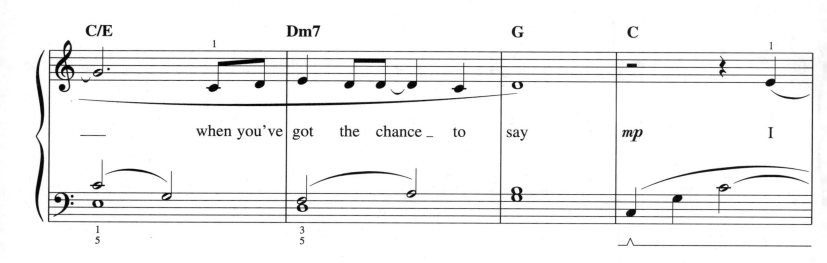

___ when you've got the chance _ to say *mp* I

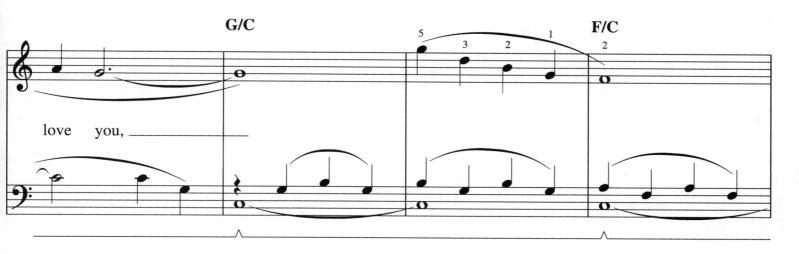

love you, _____

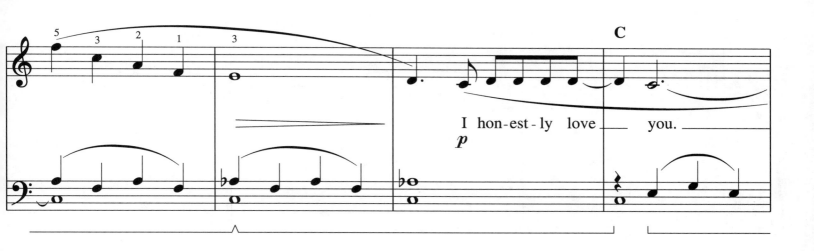

I hon-est-ly love ____ you. ____

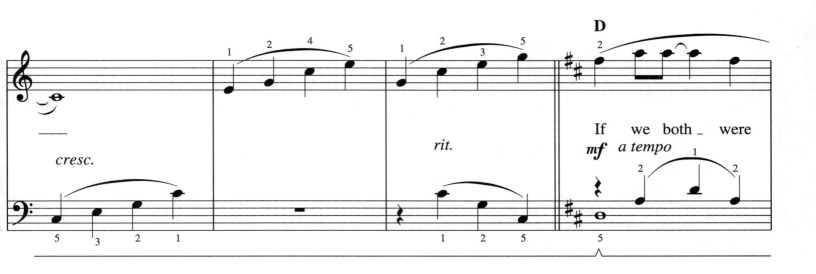

cresc.

rit.

If we both __ were

a tempo

26

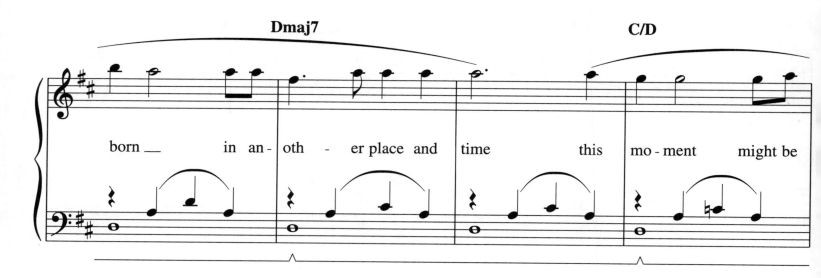

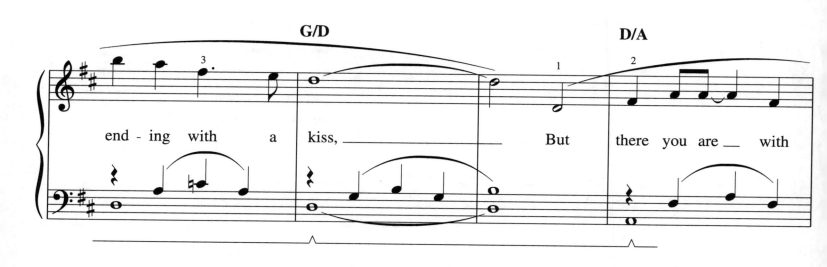

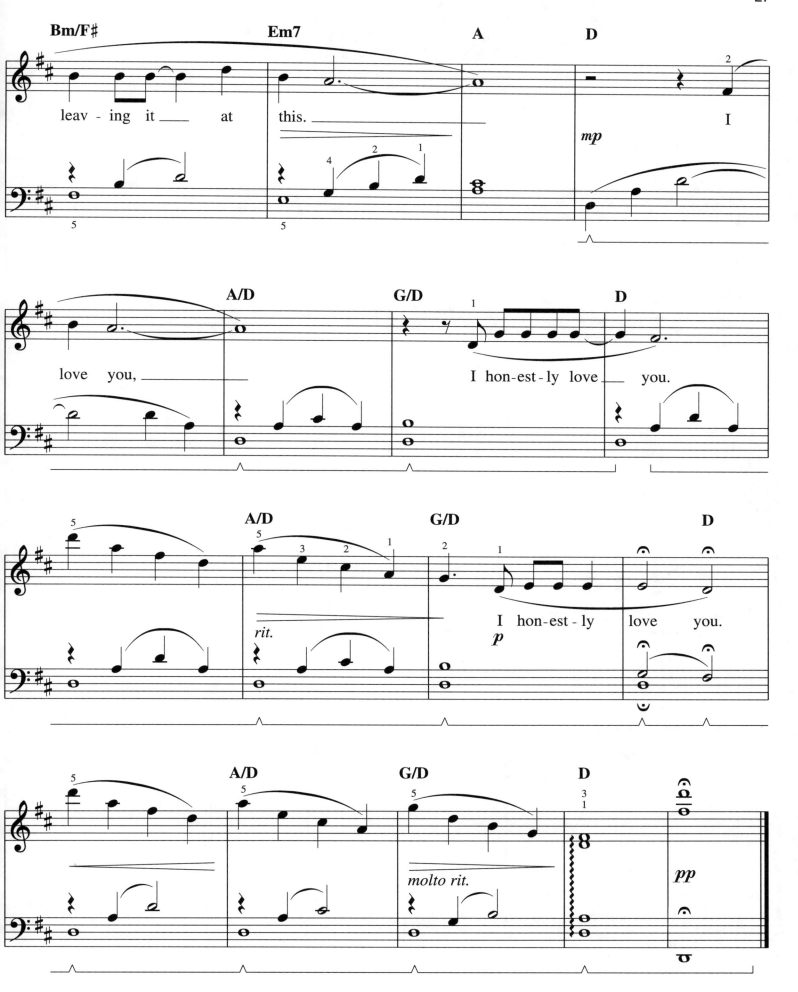

THE FIRST TIME EVER I SAW YOUR FACE

Words and Music by
EWAN MacCOLL
Arranged by Phillip Keveren

Gently flowing

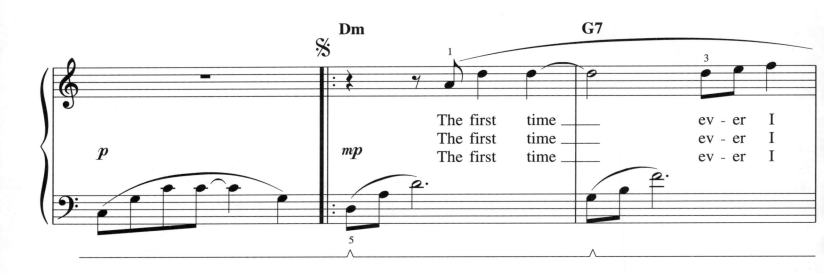

The first time ____ ev - er I
The first time ____ ev - er I
The first time ____ ev - er I

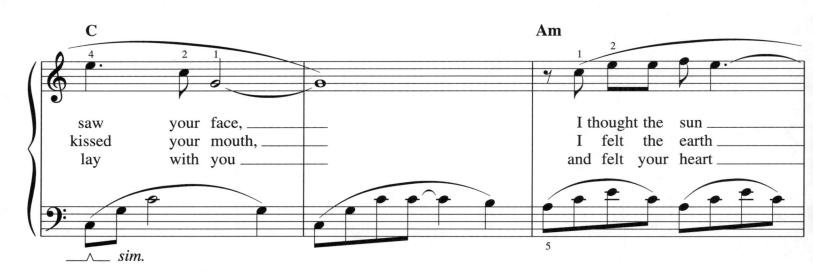

saw your face, _____
kissed your mouth, _____
lay with you _____

I thought the sun ____
I felt the earth ____
and felt your heart ____

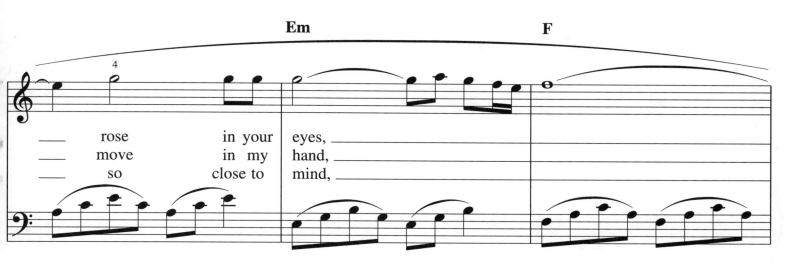

rose in your eyes,
move in my hand,
so close to mind,

And the moon and the stars were the
Like the trem - bling heart of a
And I knew our joy would

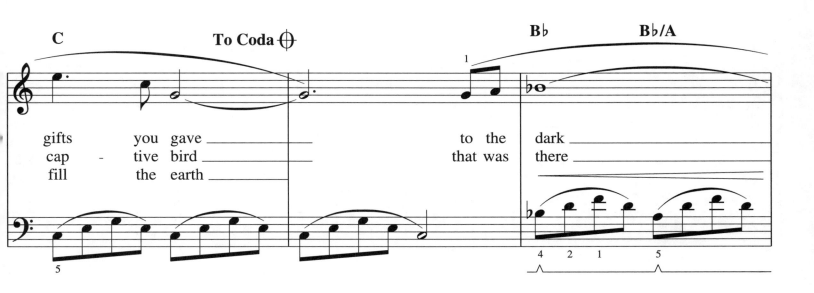

To Coda ⊕

gifts you gave to the dark
cap - tive bird that was there
fill the earth

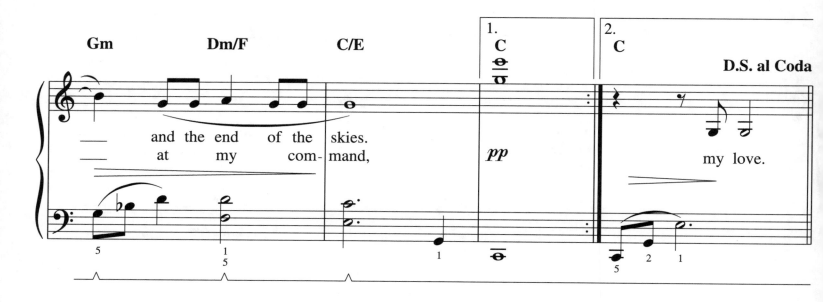

and the end   of the   skies.
at   my   com- mand,

pp

my love.

D.S. al Coda

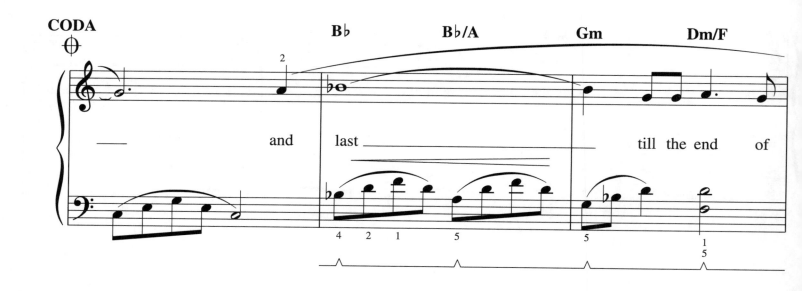

CODA

and   last _____ till the end   of

time, _____   my love. __   The first   time __

p

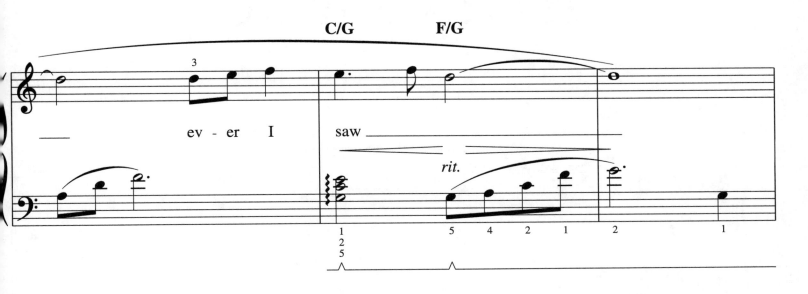

C/G   F/G

ev - er I   saw _____

rit.

C   B♭   C

your face, _   your face, _   your face, _____

pp   poco a poco cresc.
a tempo

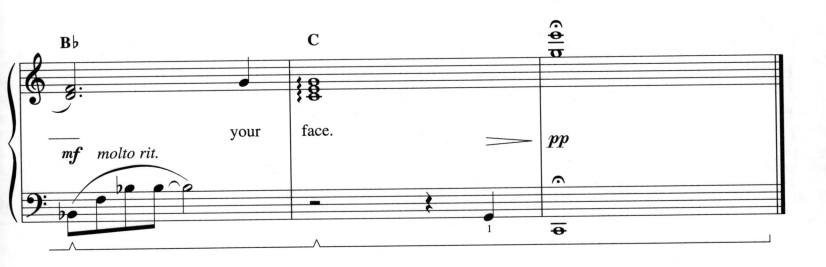

B♭   C

_ your   face.

mf   molto rit.   *pp*

FROM A DISTANCE

Words and Music by
JULIE GOLD
Arranged by Phillip Keveren

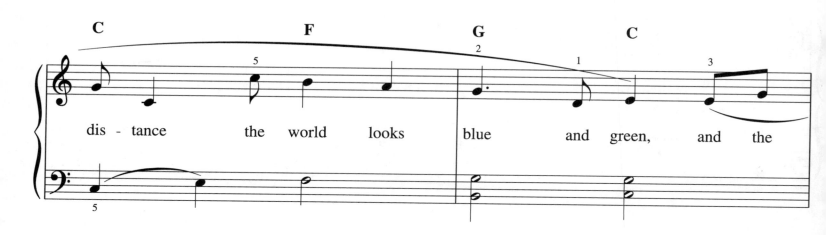

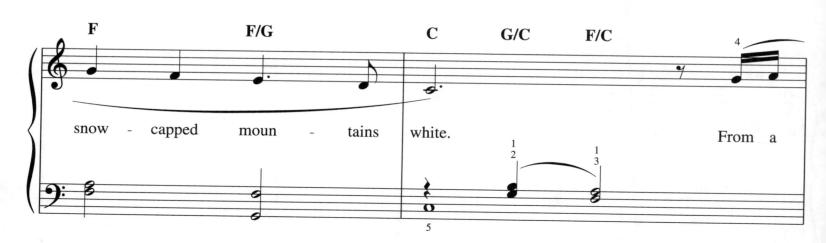

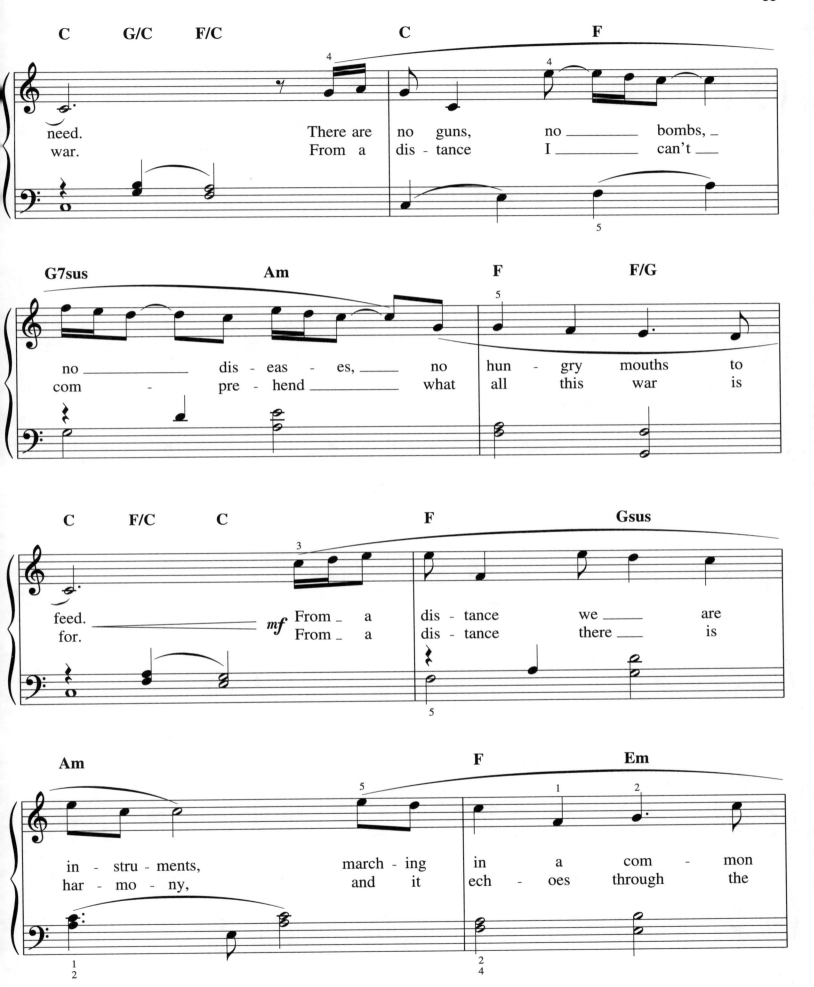

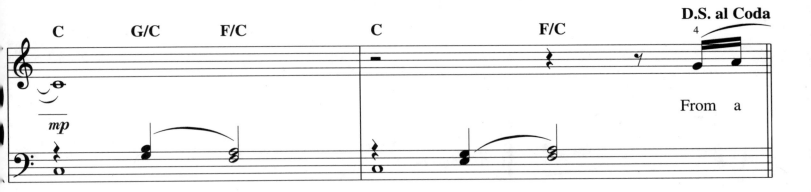

From a

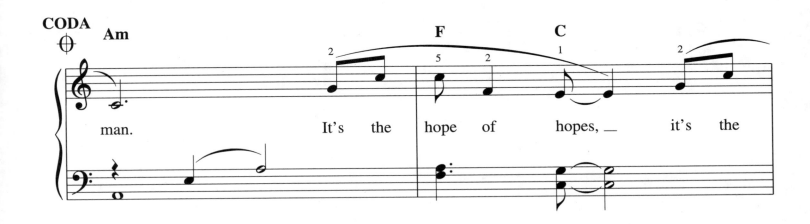

man. It's the hope of hopes, — it's the

love of loves, — it's the song of ev - 'ry

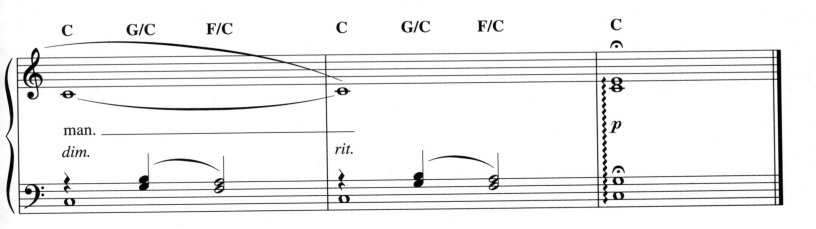

man. _____

dim.   rit.

GOODBYE TO LOVE

Words and Music by RICHARD CARPENTER
and JOHN BETTIS
Arranged by Phillip Keveren

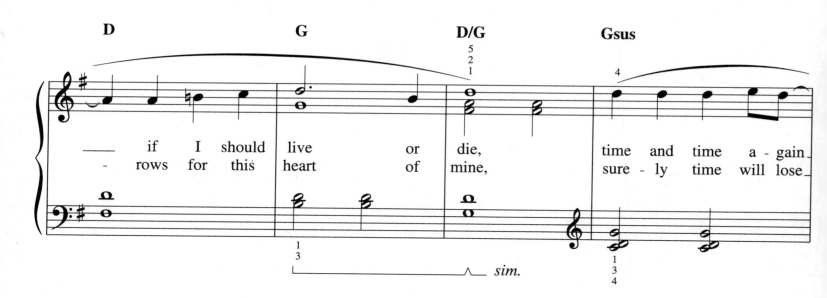

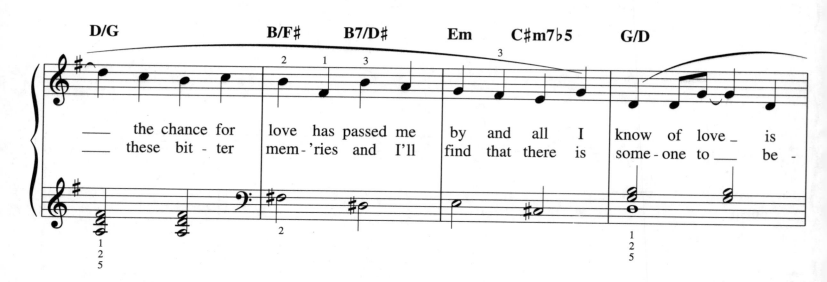

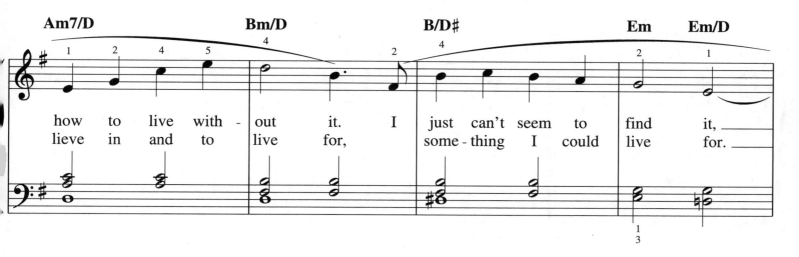

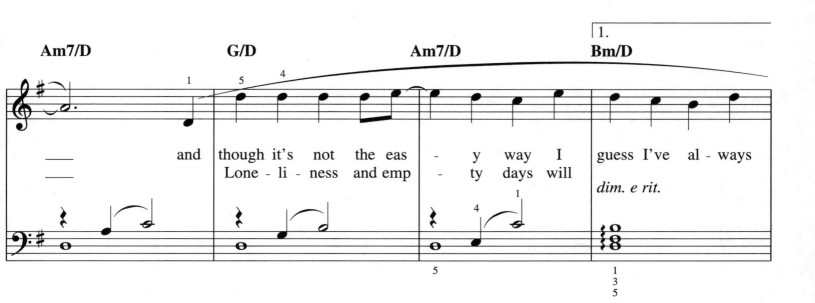

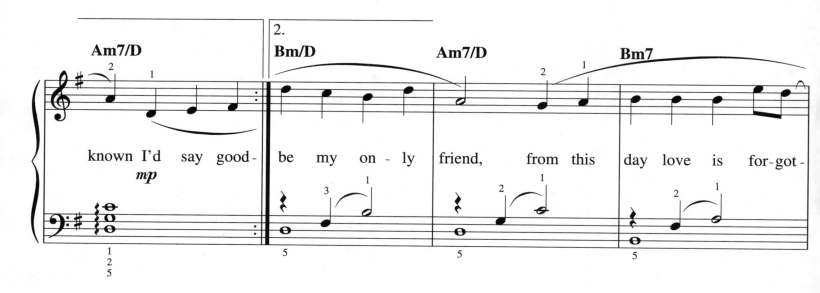

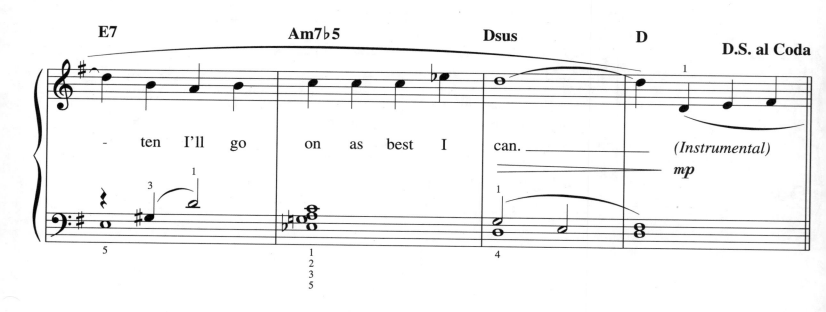

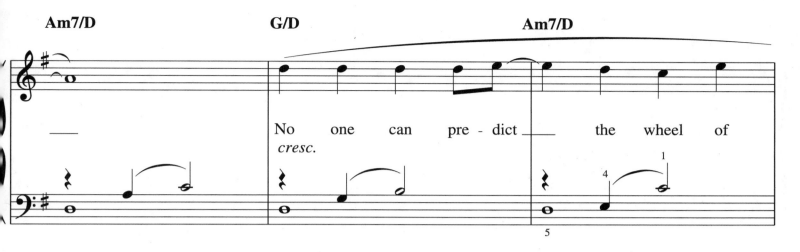

No one can pre - dict ____ the wheel of

cresc.

for - tune as it falls, There may come a time ____ when I will

f

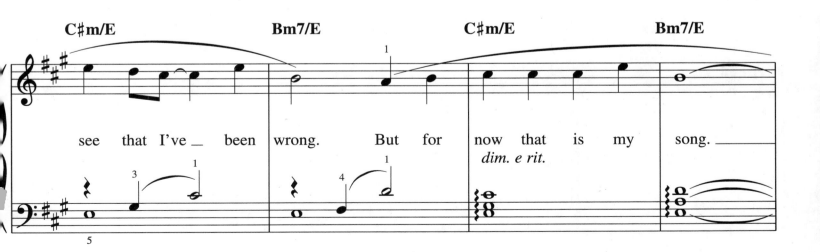

see that I've ____ been wrong. But for now that is my song. ____

dim. e rit.

I CAN'T MAKE YOU LOVE ME

Words and Music by MIKE REID
and ALLEN SHAMBLIN
Arranged by Phillip Keveren

Moderate Ballad

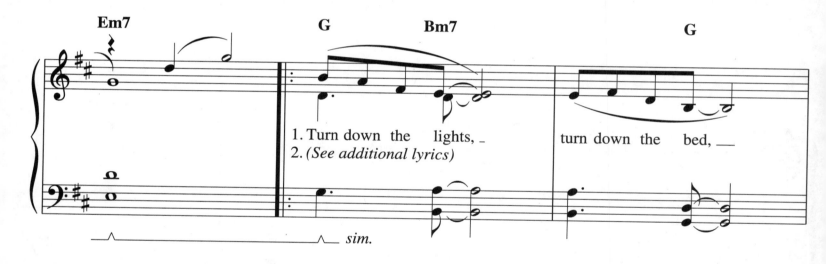

1. Turn down the lights, _
2. (See additional lyrics)

turn down the bed, _

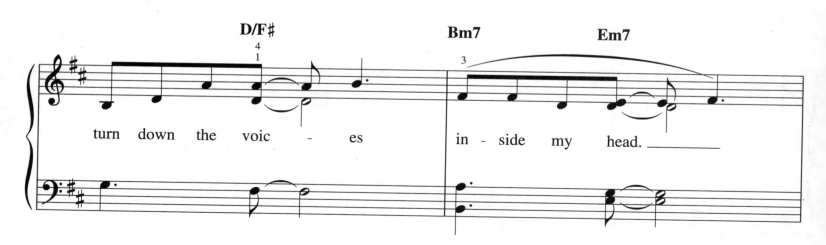

turn down the voic - es

in - side my head. _

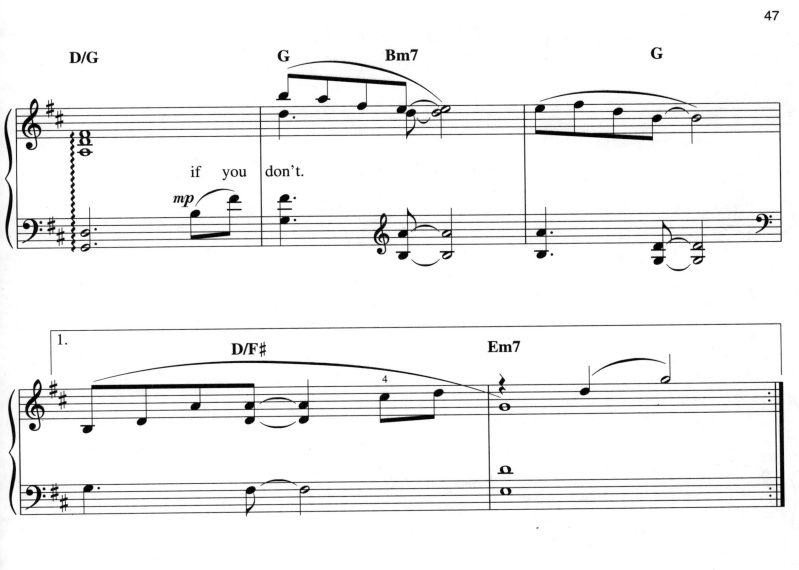

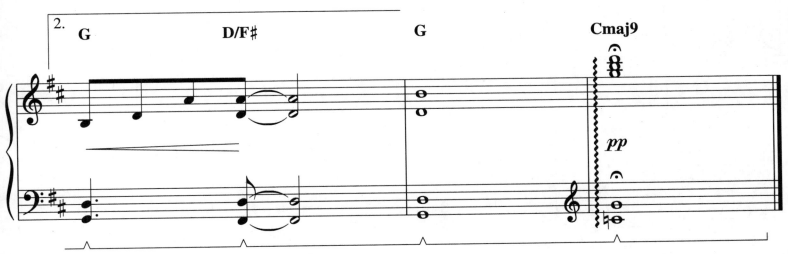

Additional Lyrics

2. I'll close my eyes, then I won't see
   The love you don't feel when you're holdin' me.
   Mornin' will come and I'll do what's right.
   Just give me till then to give up this fight.
   And I will give up this fight.
   (To Chorus:)

I WILL REMEMBER YOU

Theme from THE BROTHERS McMULLEN

Words and Music by SARAH McLACHLAN,
SEAMUS EGAN and DAVE MERENDA
Arranged by Phillip Keveren

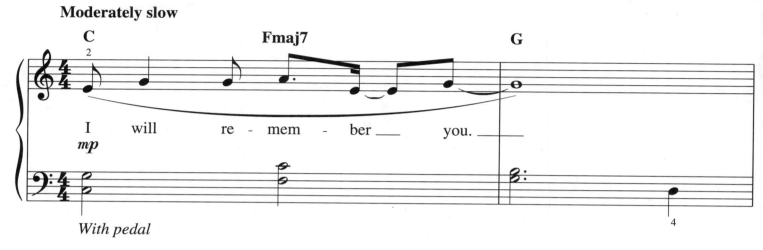

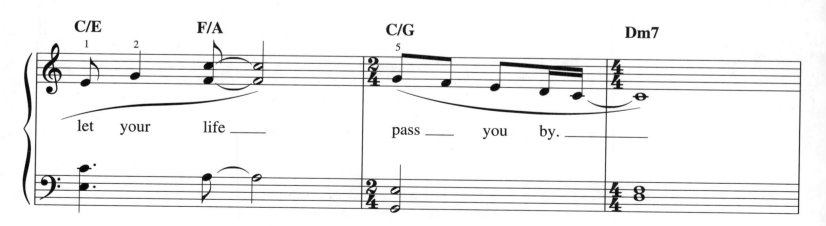

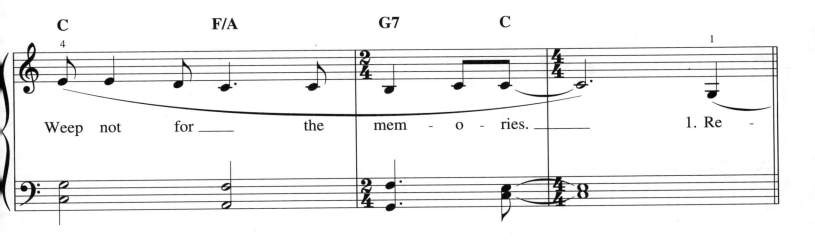

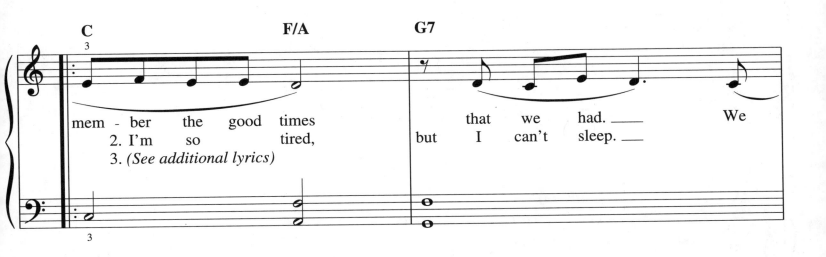

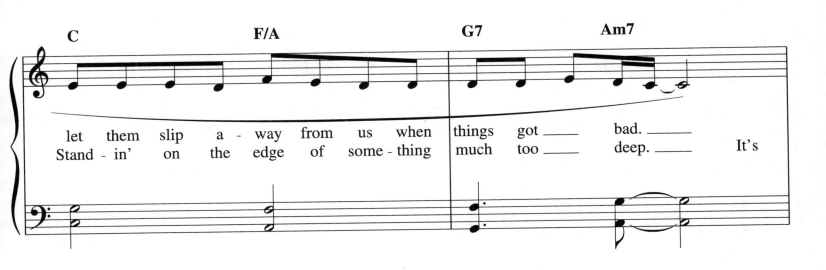

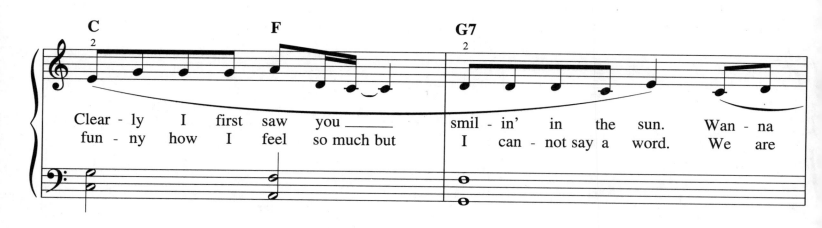

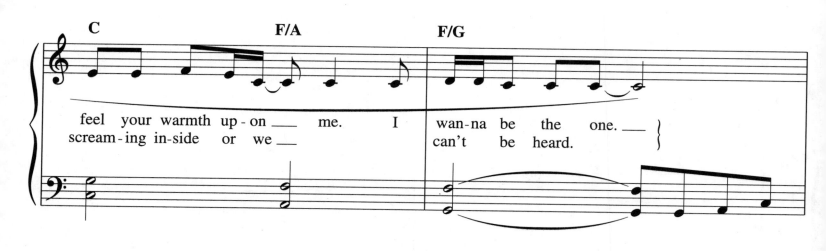

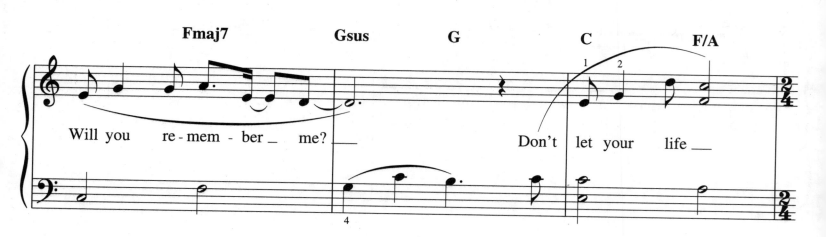

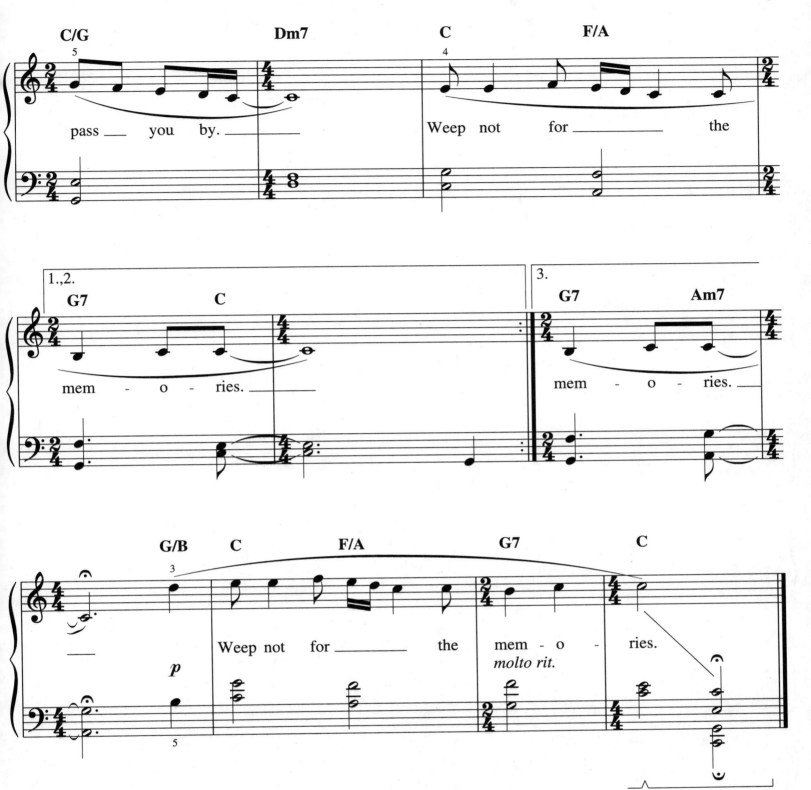

Additional Lyrics

3. I'm so afraid to love you, more afraid to lose,
Clinging to a past that doesn't let me choose.
Well once there was a darkness, a deep and endless night.
You gave me ev'rything you had, oh you gave me light.

I WRITE THE SONGS

Words and Music by
BRUCE JOHNSTON
Arranged by Phillip Keveren

Slow Ballad

I've been a - live   for - ev - er,
My home lies deep   with - in you

and I wrote the ver - y first   song.
and I've got my own place in your   soul.

I   put the words and the
Now, when I look out

young girls   cry; ___

I   write   the   songs, ___   I   write   the   songs. ___

1.

2.   *with energy*

Oh,   my   mu - sic makes you   dance _____ and gives you

spir - it   to take   a   chance,

and   I wrote some rock 'n' roll   so

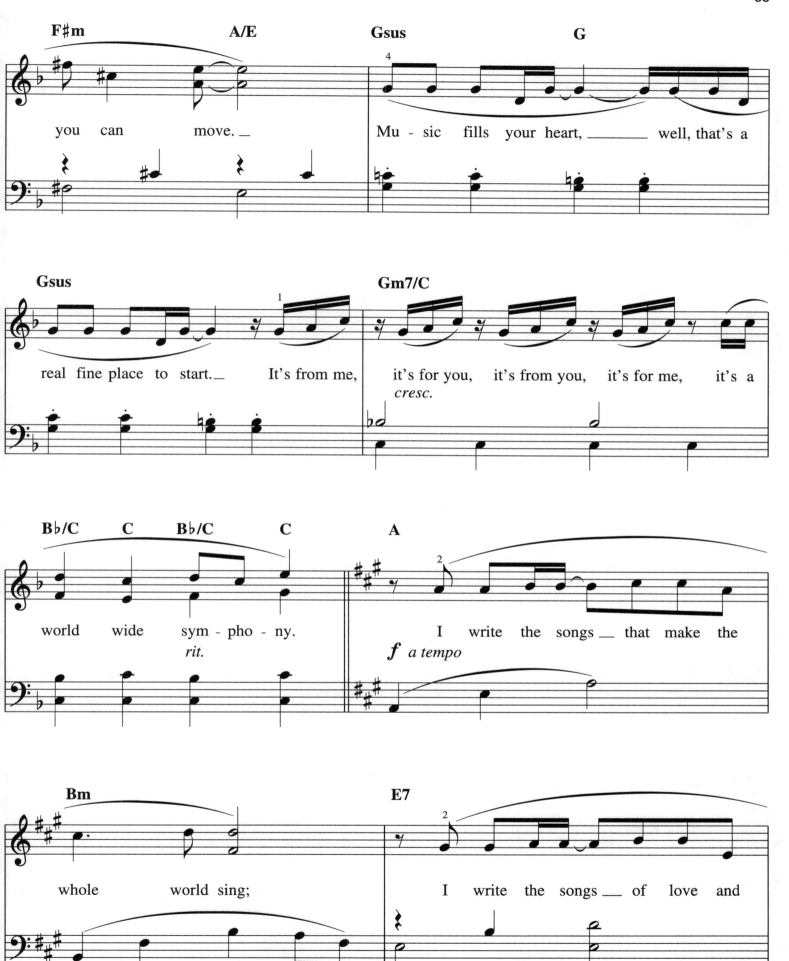

56

LOOKS LIKE WE MADE IT

Words and Music by RICHARD KERR
and WILL JENNINGS
Arranged by Phillip Keveren

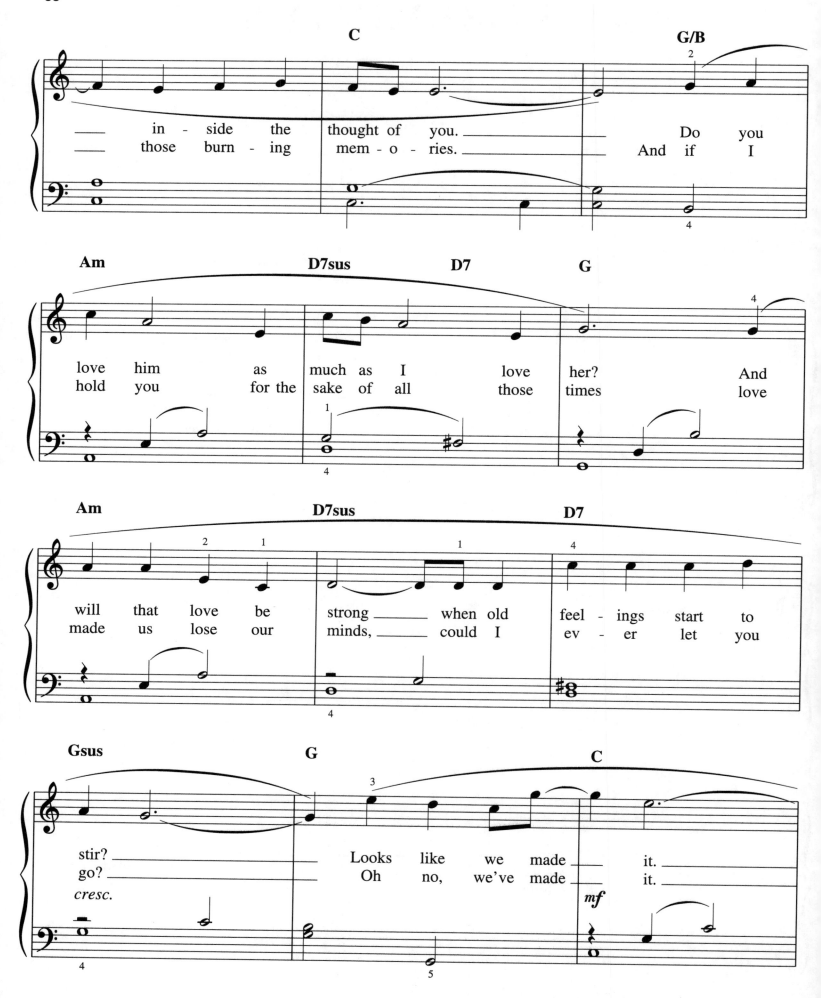

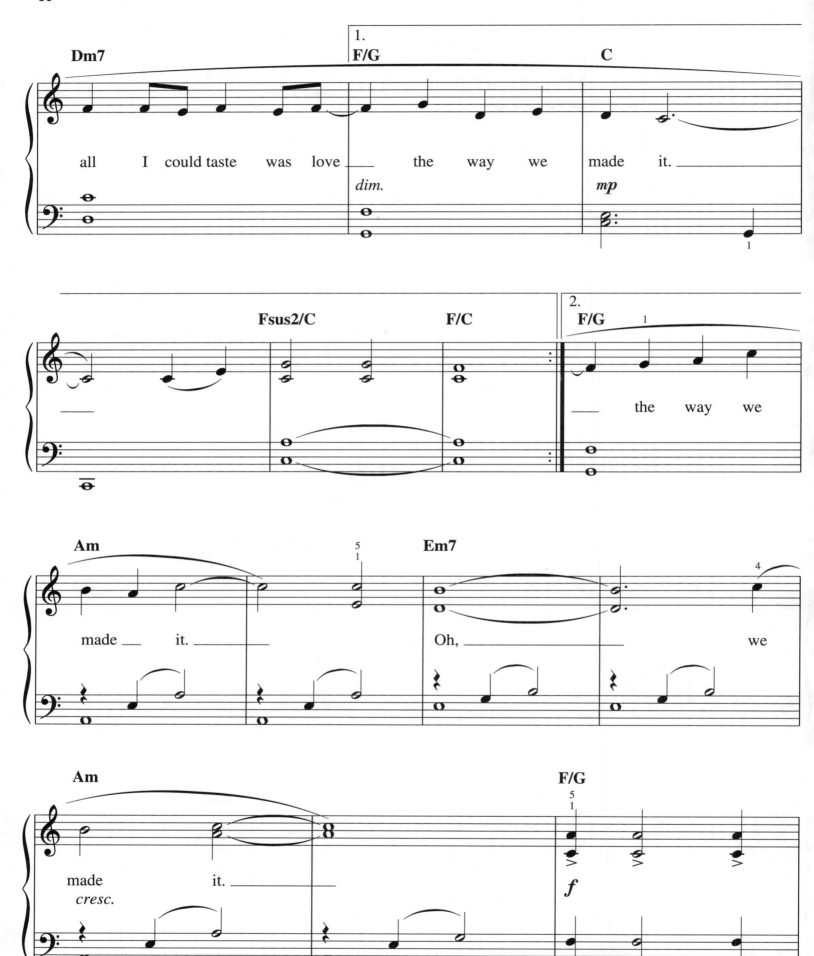

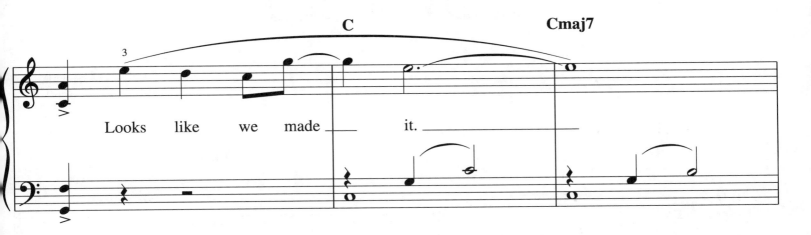

Looks like we made ___ it. ___

Looks like we made ___ it. ___

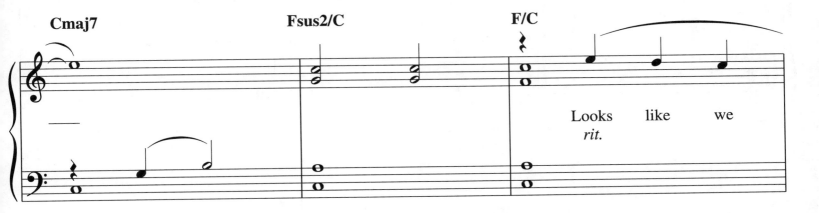

Looks like we
rit.

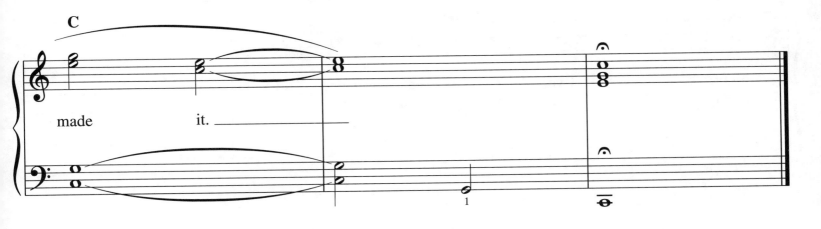

made it. ___

LADY IN RED

Words and Music by
CHRIS DeBURGH
Arranged by Phillip Keveren

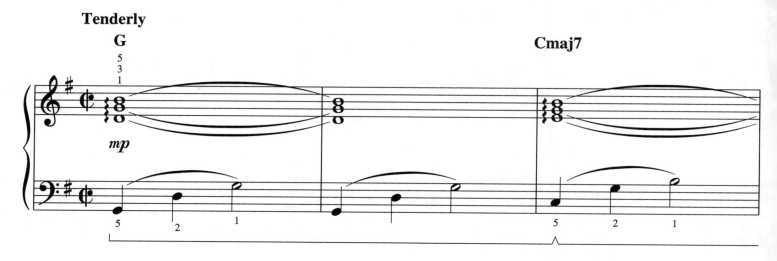

I've nev - er seen you look-ing so love - ly as you did __ to -
nev - er seen you look-ing so gor - geous as you did __ to -

night; I've nev - er seen you shine so bright. __
night; I've nev - er seen you shine so bright. __

sim.

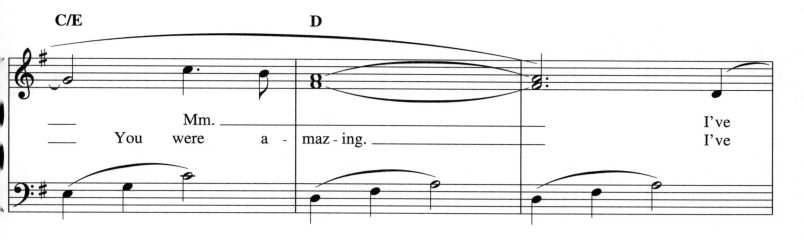

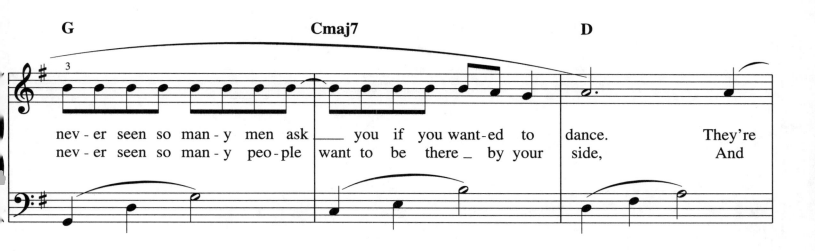

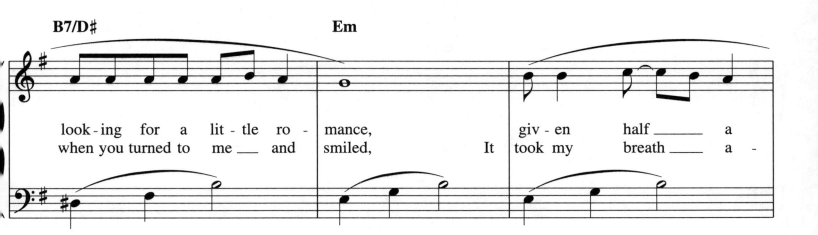

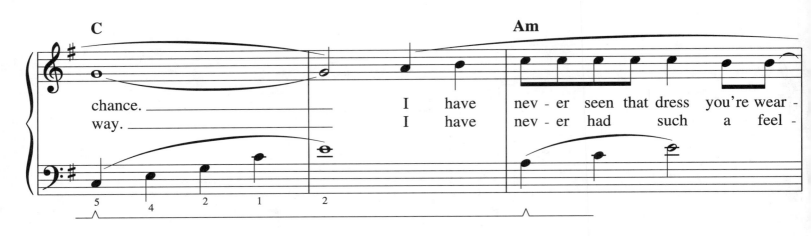

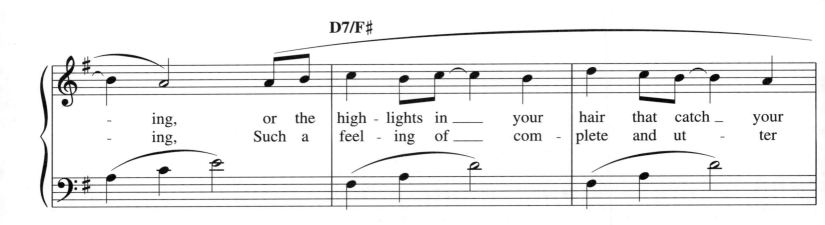

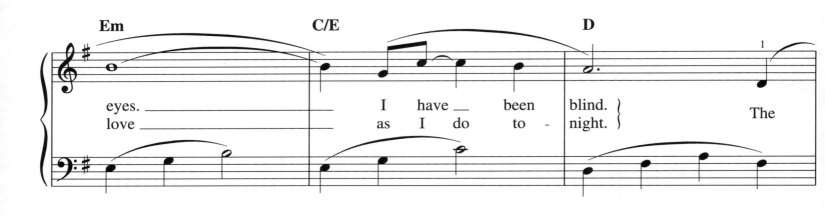

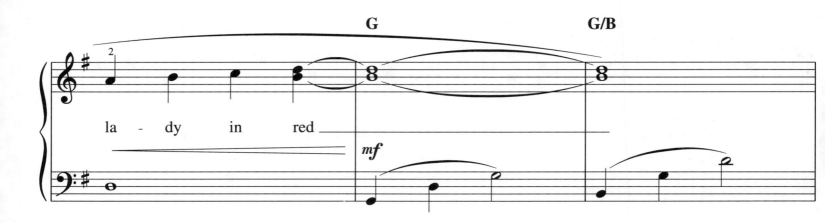

66

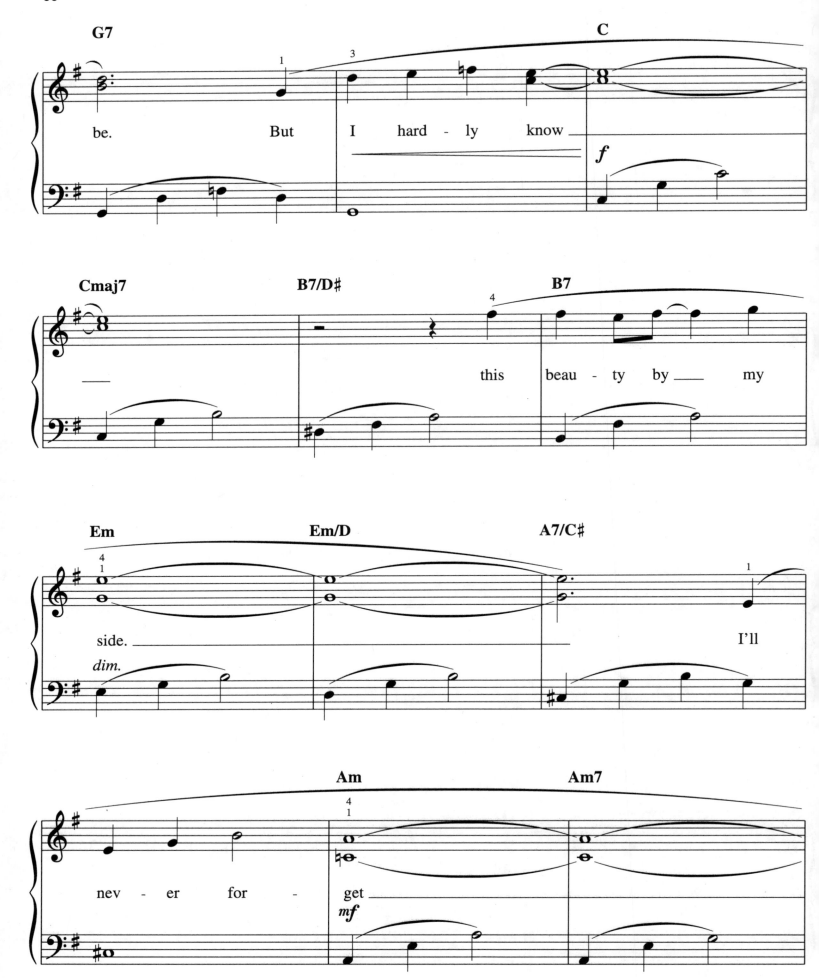

MY HEART WILL GO ON

(Love Theme from 'Titanic')
from the Paramount and Twentieth Century Fox Motion Picture TITANIC

Music by JAMES HORNER
Lyric by WILL JENNINGS
Arranged by Phillip Keveren

Moderately flowing

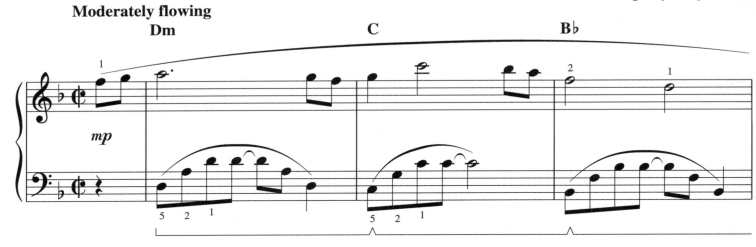

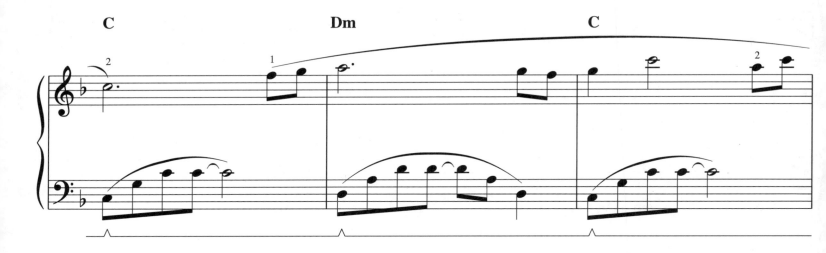

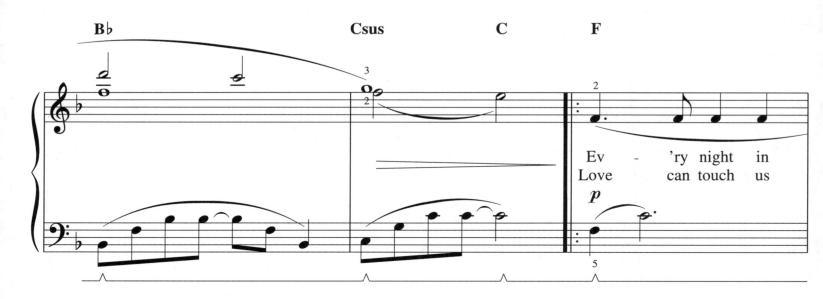

Ev - 'ry night in
Love can touch us

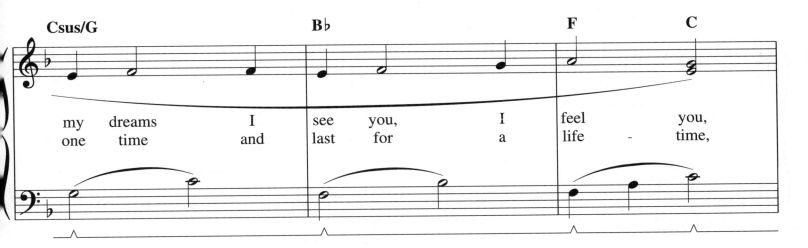

my dreams I see you, I feel you,
one time and last for a life - time,

that is how I know you go on.
and nev - er let go you 'til we're gone.

Far a - cross the dis - tance and
Love was when I loved you; one

mp

sim.

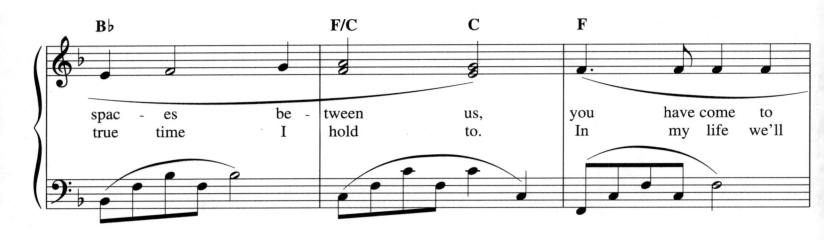

spac - es be - tween us, you have come to
true time I hold to. In my life we'll

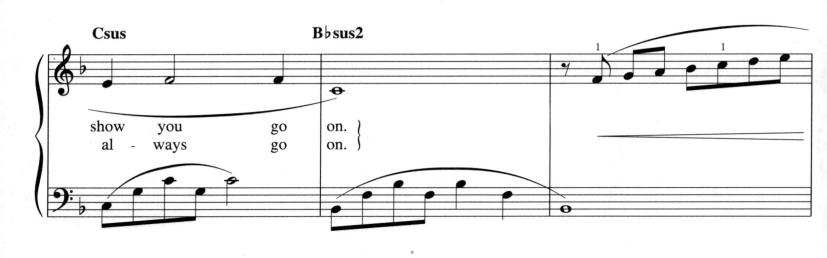

show you go on.
al - ways go on. }

Near, far, wher - ev - er you

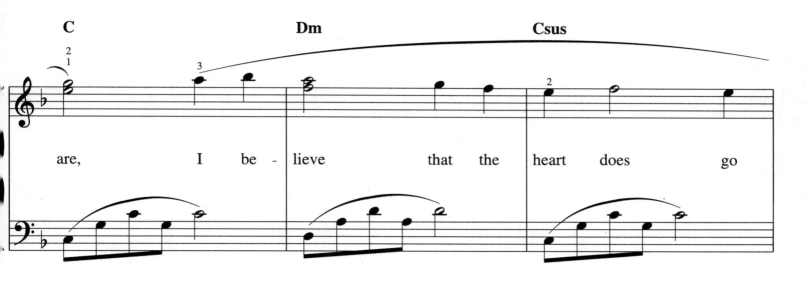

are, I be - lieve that the heart does go

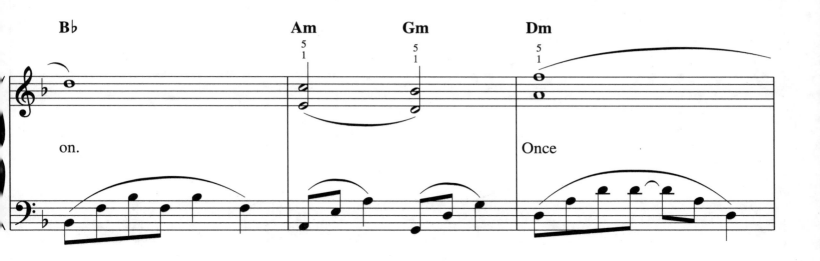

on. Once

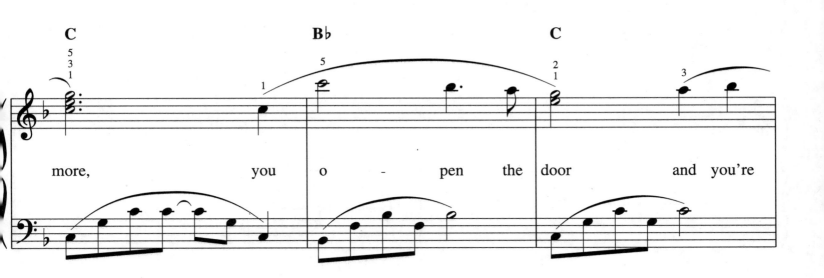

more, you o - pen the door and you're

NADIA'S THEME

from THE YOUNG AND THE RESTLESS

By BARRY DeVORZON and PERRY BOTKIN, JR.
Arranged by Phillip Keveren

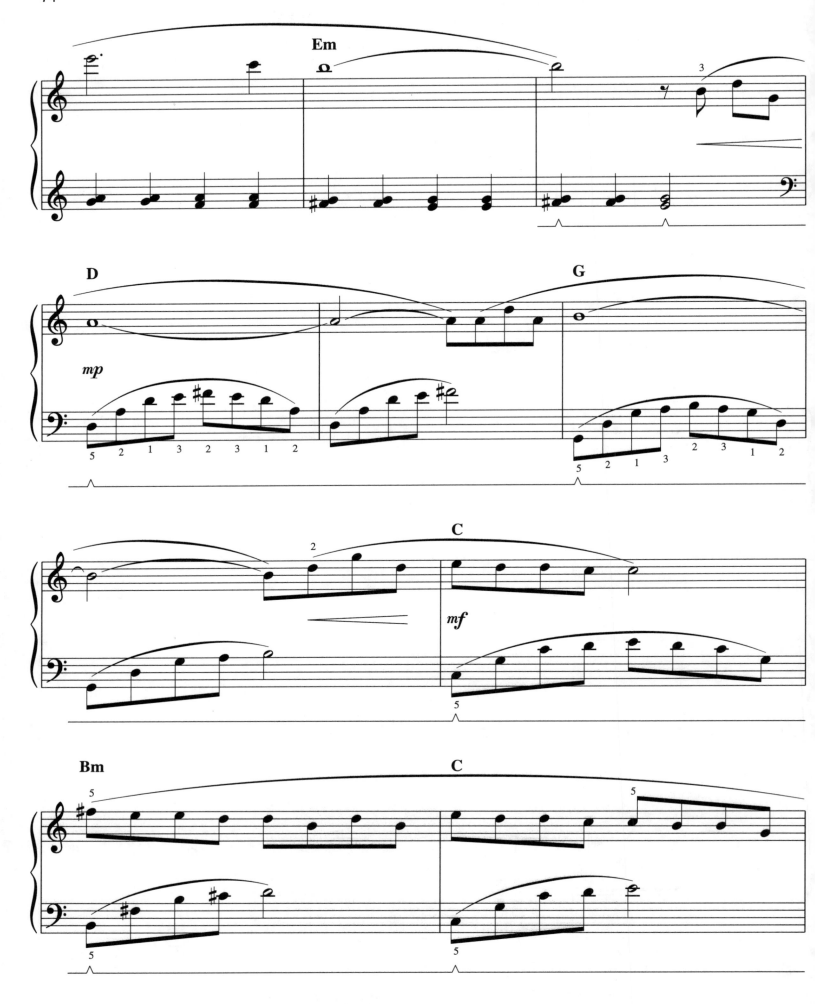

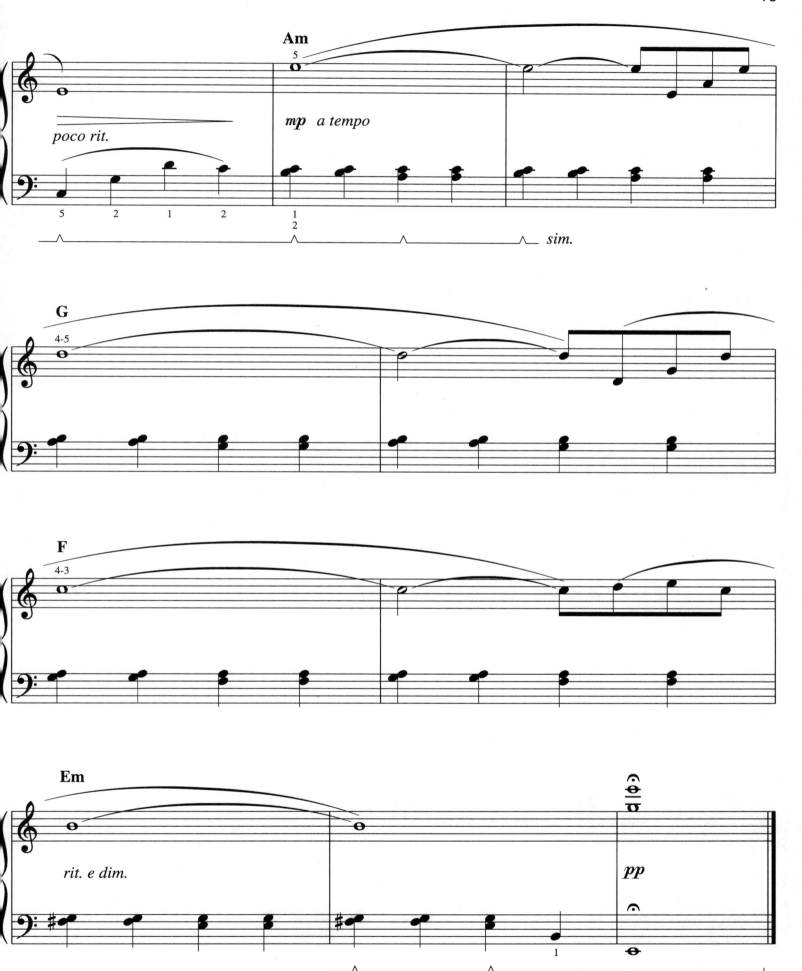

RAINDROPS KEEP FALLIN'
ON MY HEAD

Lyric by HAL DAVID
Music by BURT BACHARACH
Arranged by Phillip Keveren

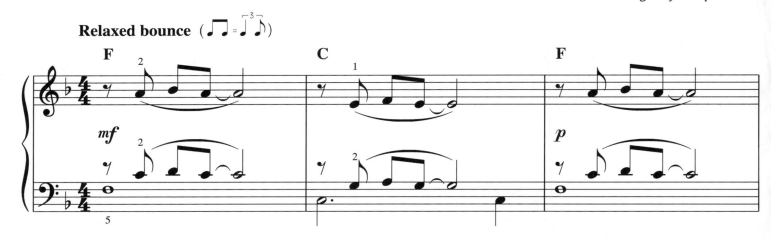

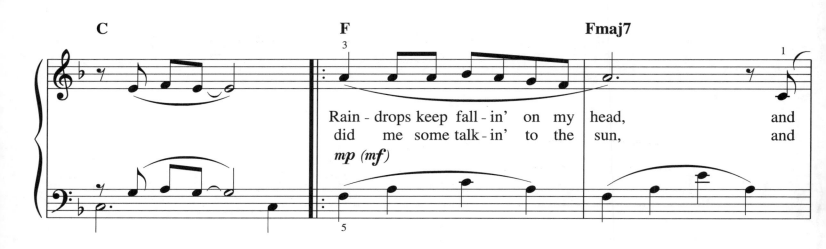

Rain - drops keep fall - in' on my head, and
did me some talk - in' to the sun, and

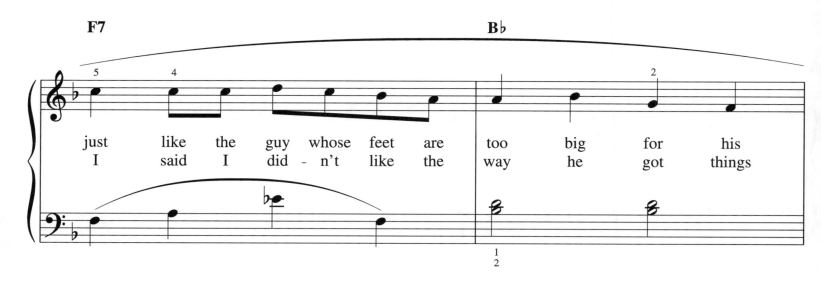

just like the guy whose feet are too big for his
I said I did – n't like the way he got his things

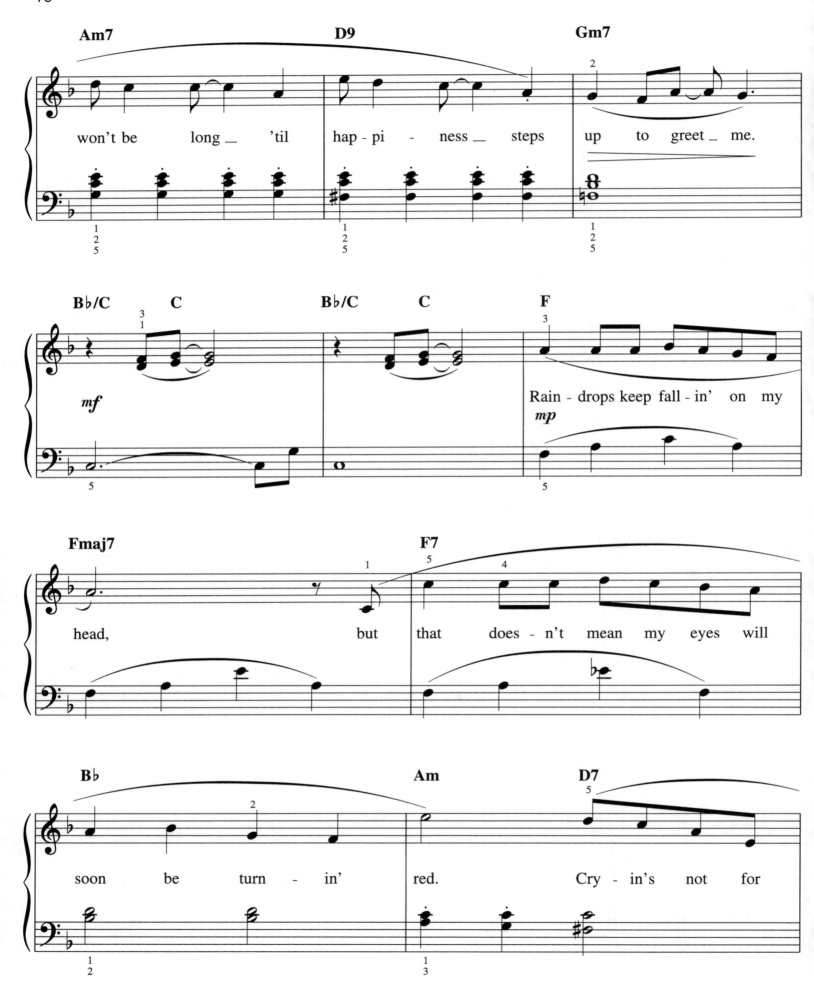

THE WAY WE WERE

from the Motion Picture THE WAY WE WERE

Words by ALAN and MARILYN BERGMAN
Music by MARVIN HAMLISCH
Arranged by Phillip Keveren

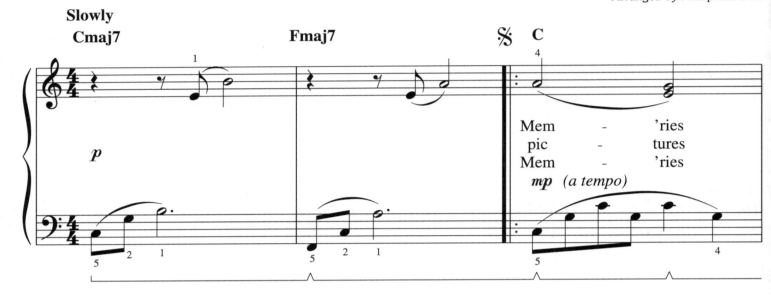

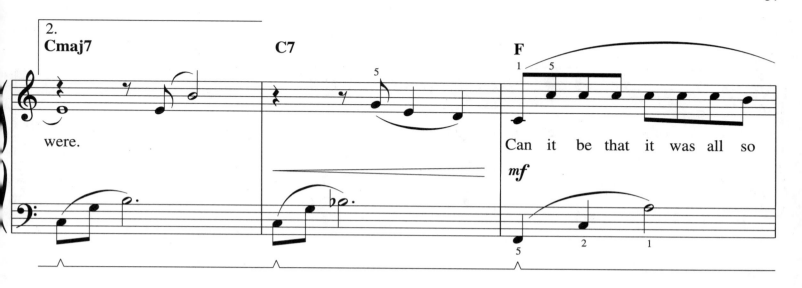

2.

Cmaj7 — were.

C7

F — Can it be that it was all so *mf*

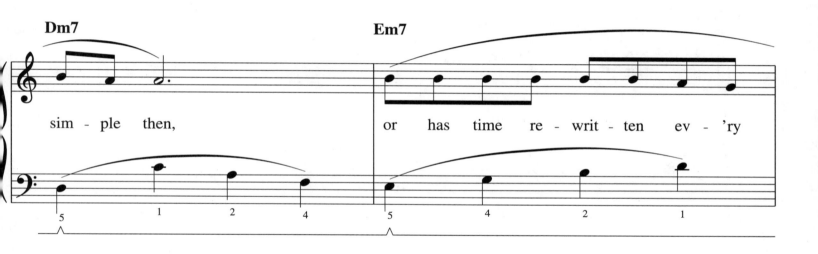

Dm7 — sim - ple then,

Em7 — or has time re - writ - ten ev - 'ry

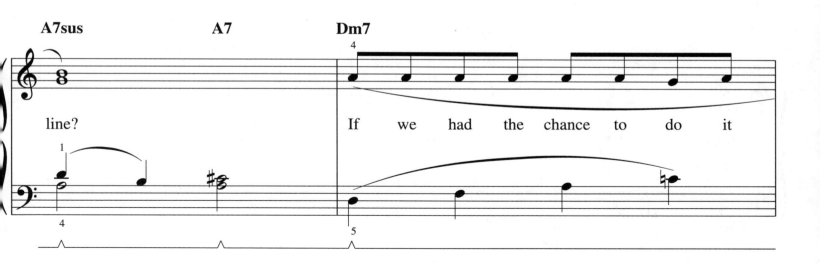

A7sus — line?

A7

Dm7 — If we had the chance to do it

D.S. al Coda

G7sus **G7** **C** **Fmaj7** **G**

all a - gain, tell me would we? ___ Could we? ___

dim. *poco rit.*

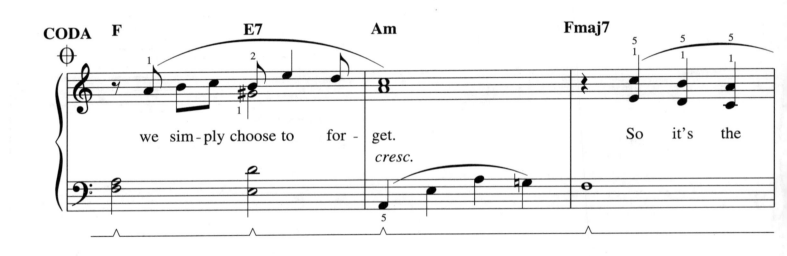

CODA **F** **E7** **Am** **Fmaj7**

we sim - ply choose to for - get. So it's the

cresc.

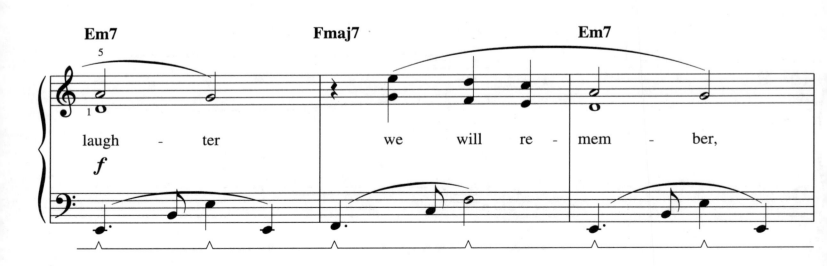

Em7 **Fmaj7** **Em7**

laugh - ter we will re - mem - ber,

f

G7sus **G7** **C** **Am** **Fmaj7**

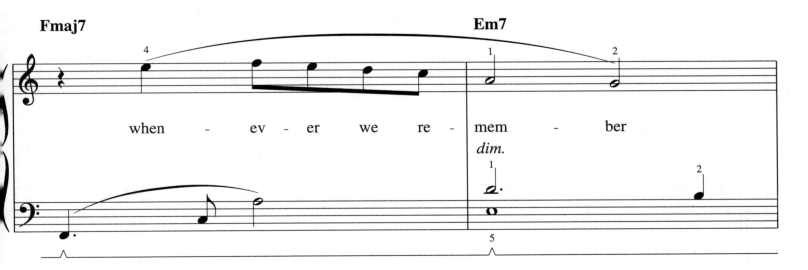

Fmaj7   Em7

when - ev - er we re - mem - ber
dim.

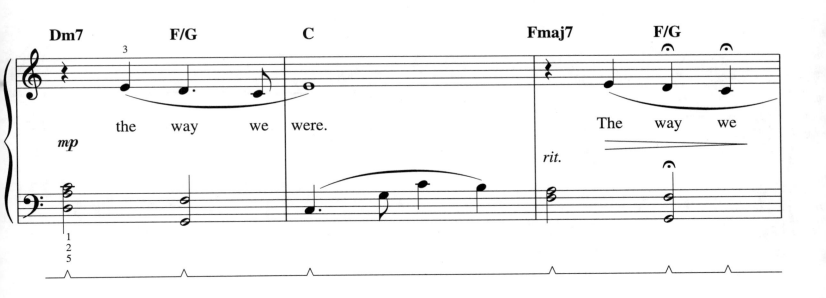

Dm7   F/G   C   Fmaj7   F/G

mp the way we were.   The way we

rit.

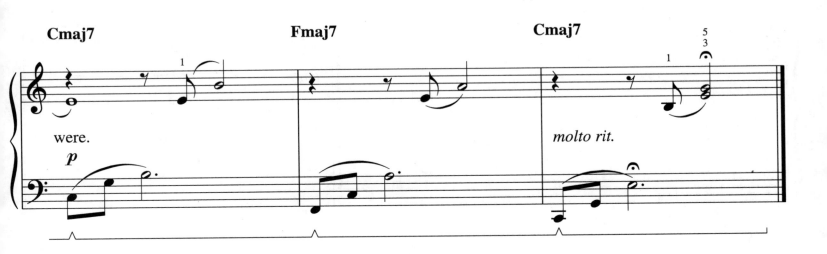

Cmaj7   Fmaj7   Cmaj7

were.   *molto rit.*

p

RAINY DAYS AND MONDAYS

Lyrics by PAUL WILLIAMS
Music by ROGER NICHOLS
Arranged by Phillip Keveren

Slowly, with melancholy

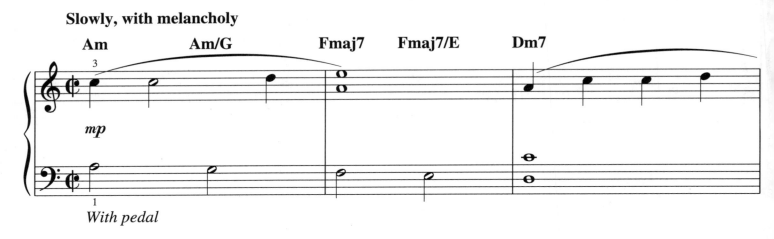

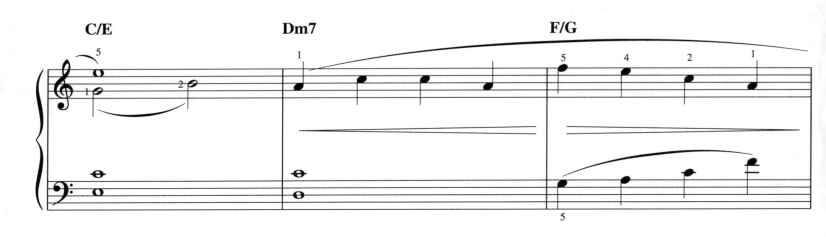

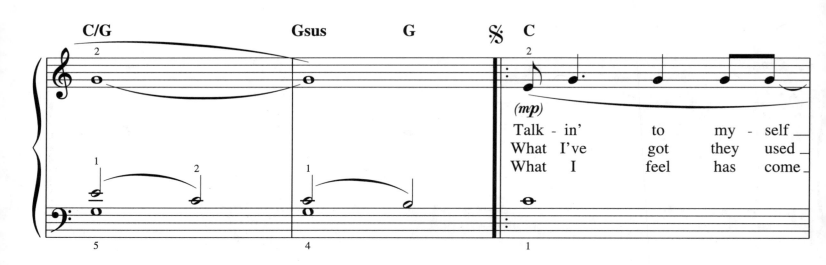

Talk - in' to my - self
What I've got they used
What I feel has come

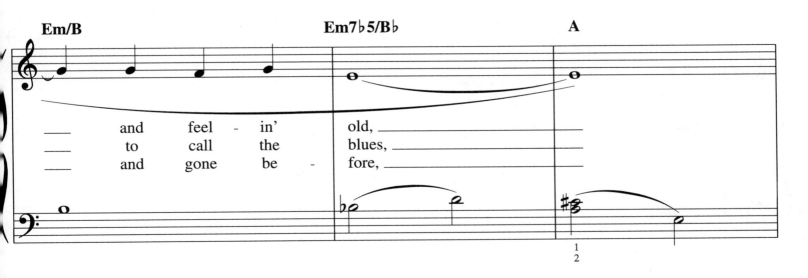

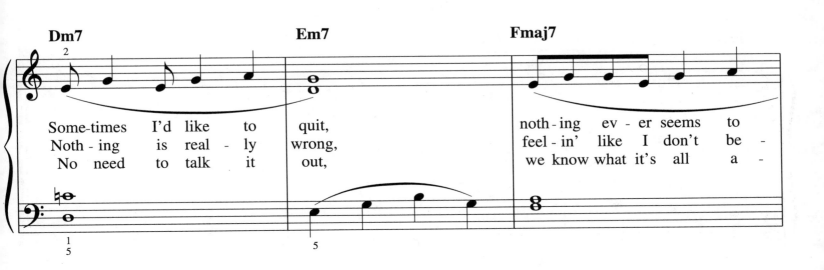

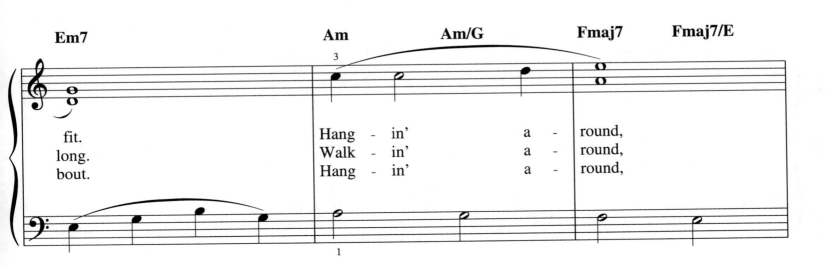

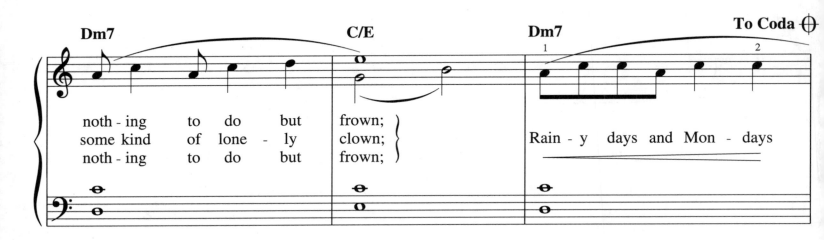

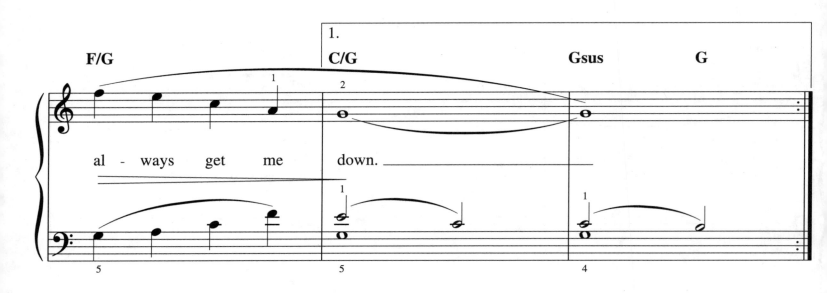

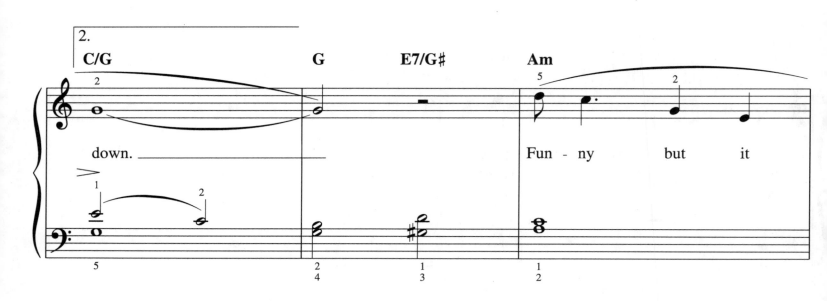

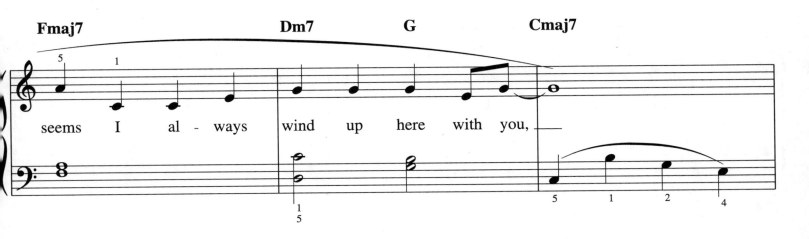

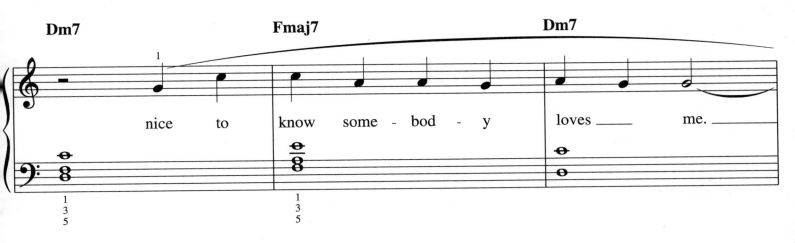

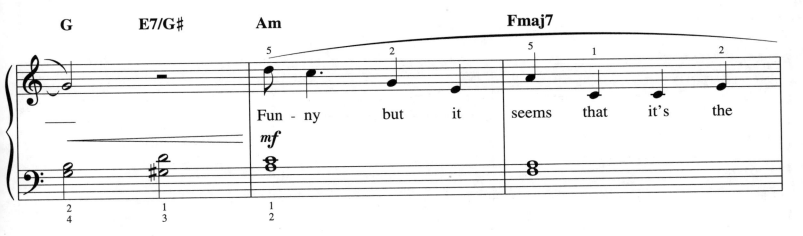

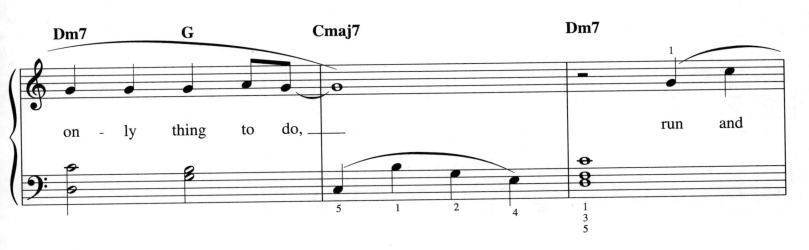

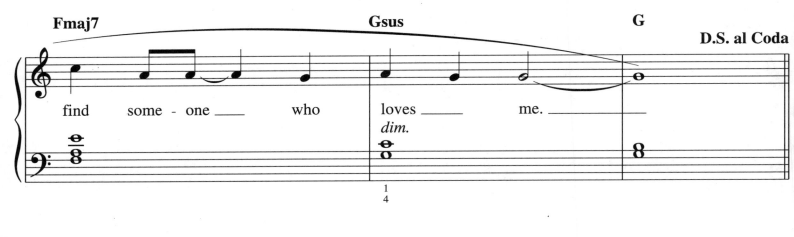

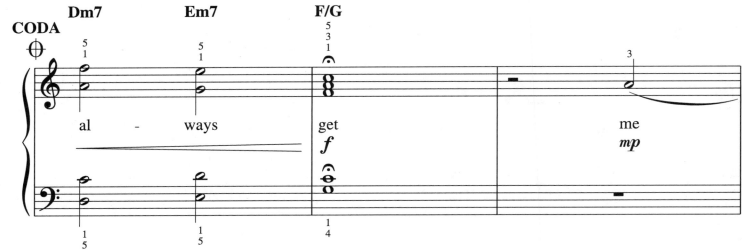

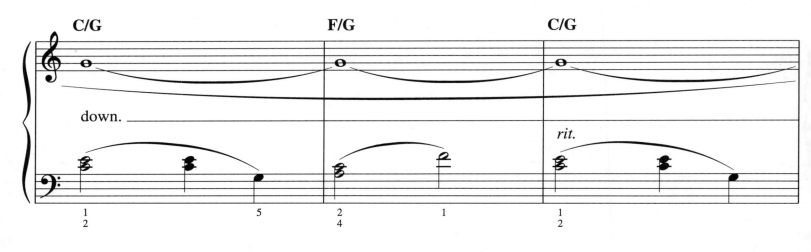

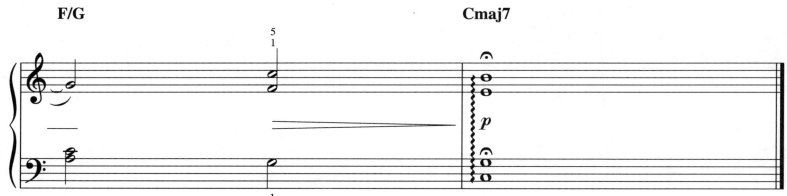